THE ETHICS OF EUTHANASIA

Other books in the At Issue series:

THE ETHICS OF EUTHANASIA

Nancy Harris, *Book Editor*

Bruce Glassman, *Vice President*
Bonnie Szumski, *Publisher*
Helen Cothran, *Managing Editor*

San Diego • Detroit • New York • San Francisco • Cleveland
New Haven, Conn. • Waterville, Maine • London • Munich

For more information, contact
Greenhaven Press
27500 Drake Rd.
Farmington Hills, MI 48331-3535
Or you can visit our Internet site at http://www.gale.com

LIBRARY OF CONGRESS CATALOGING-IN-PUBLICATION DATA

The ethics of euthanasia / Nancy Harris, book editor.
   p. cm. — (At issue)
Includes bibliographical references and index.
ISBN 0-7377-2184-7 (lib. : alk. paper) — ISBN 0-7377-2185-5 (pbk. : alk. paper)
   1. Euthanasia—Moral and ethical aspects. 2. Assisted suicide—Moral and ethical aspects. 3. Right to die—Moral and ethical aspects. I. Harris, Nancy, 1952– . II. At issue (San Diego, Calif.)
R726.E7753 2005
179.7—dc22   2003062481

Contents

Introduction

Andrea, an attractive thirty-nine-year-old woman, has been dealing with cancer for five years. She has gone through chemotherapy and radiation, procedures with severe side effects that debilitated her for months and seemed to have aged her by ten years. She has, nevertheless, recuperated enough to return to her job as director of her city's planning commission. However, Andrea's latest medical exam revealed that the cancer had spread to her bones and brain. Her oncologist has recommended further radiation treatments and chemotherapy, as well as a bone marrow transplant. Andrea is now facing even more torturous treatments as well as a very poor survival rate. After agonizing deliberation, Andrea confides in her physician that she is tired and sick of fighting, and that she wants his help to end her life. She has no living relatives to help her except a brother with whom she has no communication. Because she fears the loss of control that will inevitably come as the cancer spreads in her brain, she is asking her physician, Dr. Stanley, whom she has chosen for his caring and compassionate disposition, that when the proper time comes, he prescribe a lethal dose of medication for her. If she is not able to self-administer the drugs, she is asking that he do it for her. Andrea is looking ahead and planning what she hopes will be a peaceful and calm death. Because she is still fully functioning at work and making competent decisions, she does not feel that her request is being clouded by depression; instead, she feels that she is being realistic and hoping for a good death.

Dr. Stanley has discontinued life support at other patients' requests as well as withheld useless treatment for patients, also at their request. Both of these practices are called passive voluntary euthanasia and are legal. However, Andrea's request is something new for him. Prescribing a lethal medication for Andrea to self-administer would be physician-assisted suicide. If Dr. Stanley administered the lethal dose himself, it would be active voluntary euthanasia. Both of these practices are illegal in every state except Oregon. Dr. Stanley has a dilemma on his hands: He believes that no human should directly and intentionally take the life of another; he also wishes to relieve Andrea's suffering.

The above fictional scenario gets to the crux of the euthanasia controversy. The issue is debated by people who have radically different perspectives on the essential value of human life. As clinical psychologist and researcher from The Rehabilitation Centre in Ottawa, Canada, Keith G. Wilson points out, "People who are against legalization are motivated primarily by religious or secular moral concerns, which place the sanctity of human life above other considerations. Those who are in favor of legalization are more concerned about the relief of incontrollable pain and suffering, as well as with the rights of the individual to exercise choice and control."

Supporters of euthanasia hold autonomy, individuality, and self-determination as their highest values. They believe it is the individual's right as an autonomous being to choose when and how to die. They contend that respect for an individual's rights to autonomy and self-determination is fundamental to human dignity. Some euthanasia supporters propose that the right to die is guaranteed under the law and the constitutional "right to privacy," which forbids the state from interfering in private decisions, including when to die.

In requesting assistance in dying, Andrea is exercising self-determination, individuality, and autonomy. She is also expressing another value dear to euthanasia supporters, which is the right to have a planned and peaceful death. In the face of debilitating disease, Andrea values the quality of her life more than life itself; she feels her life, so greatly compromised by her illness, will one day not be worth living. Andrea may be able to face death more calmly knowing that she has the option to end her life when she chooses, enabling her to enjoy the time she has left. As expressed by Faye Girsh, executive director of the Hemlock Society, a pro-euthanasia organization, "The reason that polls in this country, and in Canada, Australia, Great Britain, and other parts of Europe, show 60 to 80 percent support for legalization of assisted suicide is that people want to know they will have a way out if their suffering becomes too great. They dread losing control not only of their bodies but of what will happen to them in the medical system." In requesting assistance from her physician, Andrea is calling on Dr. Stanley's compassion and mercy. She, like many others in her position, is asking him to alleviate and eventually end her suffering.

Euthanasia opponents, on the other hand, believe that the sanctity of life is of supreme value. They believe that it is wrong to kill another human being through euthanasia and that suicide and physician-assisted suicide are intrinsically evil. Furthermore, in their view, euthanasia is a threat to the moral fabric of society. As expressed by professor of medicine and law Margaret Somerville, "Euthanasia presents an overt threat to maintaining the important societal value of the sanctity of life." She adds, "To legalize such killing, especially to institutionalize it in the medical profession, is to set destructive values for our society." Opponents fear that by practicing euthanasia society will become desensitized toward death resulting in the devaluation of human life.

Dr. Stanley agrees with these opponents that the sanctity of life is of supreme importance. He is also influenced by the medical profession's Hippocratic oath, which says that a physician should "give no deadly medicine to any one." For a physician to kill or assist in killing might ultimately lead to the destruction of patient-doctor trust and tarnish the image of the physician. Dr. Stanley believes that the role of the compassionate physician, acting on behalf of his patient's welfare, is to protect his patient from death. Dr. Stanley has no obligation to comply with Andrea's wishes, but he must let her know his feelings in time for her to find another physician who might help her.

As this scenario illustrates, there are strongly divergent values underlying the euthanasia controversy. Modern technology and medicine have brought these issues to the foreground. Diseases that historically would have killed people are now successfully treated. In addition, death no longer occurs mainly in the home among family but in hospitals; at least 75 percent of deaths occur in institutional settings, either nursing homes or hospitals. Usually a variety of treatments had been undertaken to forestall these deaths, resulting in increased medical decision-making near the end of the patient's life. Many people feel, as Andrea has anticipated, a profound lack of control in these new end-of-life situations. Indeed, surveys show that a large majority of people in the United States would like to be allowed to end their lives before incurable and painful diseases debilitate them and submit them to unbearable suffering. Whether they will be allowed to make this choice will depend in part on the course taken by the euthanasia debate.

The euthanasia debate will continue to be an emotional and complex one. This anthology, *At Issue: The Ethics of Euthanasia*, presents personal, medical, and religious perspectives on this hotly debated topic. How policy makers eventually address the ethical challenges surrounding euthanasia has enormous personal consequences for people like Andrea and Dr. Stanley.

1

No Ethical Difference Exists Between Active and Passive Euthanasia

Leslie Burkholder

Leslie Burkholder is an instructor in the department of philosophy at the University of British Columbia in Vancouver, Canada.

There is no ethical distinction between passive euthanasia, where treatment is withheld or withdrawn from a patient who then dies, or active euthanasia, where a physician gives a lethal dose of medication to end a patient's life. A slippery slope argument can be used to support this perspective. If, for example, it is ethical to turn off a ventilator keeping alive a terminally ill patient, then it would be moral to turn off a similar patient's artificial lungs, even though they were located within her body while the first patient's ventilator was outside her body. There is no moral distinction between these cases. By the same logic, if it is acceptable to remove life support from these two patients—because the difference between their cases is a factual, not a moral one—then it is also ethical to inject a chemical agent into a similar patient kept alive with artificial lungs. Although the action in this case is delivering a death-causing agent rather than turning off a patient's lungs, again, this is merely a factual difference, not a moral one. Last, if there is no moral difference between turning off a patient's artificial lungs and stopping them with a chemical agent, there is no moral distinction between delivering that agent, which ultimately causes death, and administering a fatal dose of morphine to another patient.

Many medical professionals and ordinary people still think there is generally or always a morally significant difference between passive euthanasia and active euthanasia. On the one hand, they think that it is ethically proper for a medical professional to stop treatment, at a competent patient's request, even when the foreseen result is that the patient

Leslie Burkholder, "Nancy B and Nancy F," *Journal of Applied Philosophy*, vol. 18, no. 2, 2001. Copyright © 2001 by the Society for Applied Philosophy. Reproduced by permission of Blackwell Publishers.

will die. That is, they believe that passive euthanasia is sometimes—for instance, when it is fully voluntary—morally acceptable. On the other hand, they also believe that it is morally wrong for a medical professional to administer to a patient, even at that patient's competent request, anything which is intended to cause the patient's death. In other words, they think that active euthanasia isn't morally acceptable.

Many medical professionals and ordinary people still think there is generally or always a morally significant difference between passive euthanasia and active euthanasia.

Many or all of those who say that there is such a difference would certainly say that the following two cases are ethically quite different.

Nancy B. Nancy B had a mechanical ventilator, an artificial lung, attached to her, but outside her body. Without its continued action she would die by suffocation. She had a muscle-wasting illness; this is what had destroyed her lungs. Her medical condition would get no better and eventually would probably get worse. She saw no point in continuing to stay alive. She wanted to die by having the ventilator withdrawn or turned off. She couldn't do this by herself. Someone else, preferably a member of the hospital staff where she was staying, would have to do it for her.

Nancy F. Nancy F also had a muscle-wasting disease, although not the same one as Nancy B. Sooner or later, she would need a mechanical ventilator to allow her to breathe. But, for now, the lungs she was born with were performing their function. Her condition would fairly rapidly worsen until eventually she died. She saw no point in continuing to stay alive until then. She wanted to die now by having someone, preferably a knowledgeable medical professional, administer a dose of morphine strong enough to stop the action of her lungs. She couldn't do this by herself. Someone else would have to do it for her.

I think there is a simple argument which says that what these people believe, at least about the cases of Nancy B and Nancy F, is false. There is no moral difference between the two cases.

Intermediate imaginary cases

Consider, not merely the Nancy B and Nancy F cases, but some intermediate imaginary cases. (The Nancy B and Nancy F cases are both based on real Canadian cases. Some details of the intermediate cases are science fiction. There are no implantable artificial lungs, for example.)

Nancy C. Nancy C had mechanical ventilators, artificial lungs, inside her body. These replaced her natural lungs, which had stopped working some time ago. Without them she would have died by suffocation. She had a muscle-wasting illness; this is what had destroyed her natural lungs. Her medical condition would get no better; eventually it would be worse. She saw no point in continuing to stay alive. She wanted to die by having the artficial lungs inside her body turned off. This could be done outside her body by remote control. She couldn't do this by herself. Someone else, preferably a member of the hospital staff where she was staying, would have to do it for her.

Nancy D. Nancy D also had mechanical ventilators, artificial lungs, inside her body. These replaced her natural lungs, which had stopped working some time ago. Without them she would have died by suffocation. She had a muscle-wasting illness; this is what had destroyed her lungs. Her medical condition would never improve and it would probably get worse. She saw no point in continuing to stay alive. She wanted to die by having the artficial lungs inside her body turned off. The easiest and least painful way to do this would be to administer a dose of a chemical agent strong enough to stop the action of her implanted artificial lungs. She couldn't do this by herself. Someone else, preferably a knowledgeable medical professional, would have to do it for her.

Nancy E. Nancy E had received cadaveric lung transplants. They replaced her natural lungs, which had stopped working some time ago. Without the lung transplants or a mechanical ventilator, she would have died by suffocation. But she had a muscle-wasting illness; this is what had destroyed her original lungs and would even eventually destroy the transplants. Her medical condition would never get better; it would only get worse. She saw no point in continuing to stay alive. She wanted to die by having someone administer a dose of morphine strong enough to stop the action of her transplanted lungs. She couldn't do this by herself. Someone else, preferably a member of the hospital staff where she was staying, would have to do it for her.

Looking at the cases through reasoning

The argument or reasoning is perfectly obvious: It is a virtuous slippery slope. Suppose, to start at the top, it is definitely not wrong for a medical professional to help Nancy B die in the way she wants. (This is what many people who think there is an important difference between the cases of Nancy B and Nancy F believe.) Then it is hard to see why it shouldn't also be acceptable to assist Nancy C. The only difference is that the artificial ventilators or lungs are inside Nancy C's body. In Nancy B's case, there was an artificial ventilator but it was outside her body. Can that make a difference? It is hard to see why. But if it is morally acceptable to help Nancy C die then it must also be morally proper for a medical professional to assist Nancy D die. Again, there is a small but plain factual difference between the cases of Nancy C and Nancy D. To make Nancy D's artificial lungs stop functioning it is necessary to administer by injection a chemical that stops them from working. Their action cannot be stopped from outside her body. This hardly seems like it could make a moral difference in the present context between the cases of Nancy C and Nancy D. But then, if it is not morally wrong to help Nancy D die then it is also not morally improper to help Nancy E die either. The only difference between these two cases is that, in Nancy D's case, the ventilator is an artificial, mechanical, device implanted in her body, replacing the lungs she was born with. In Nancy E's case the lungs are natural lungs, although not the ones she was born with. Could that make a moral difference? It is difficult to see why. So the Nancy D and Nancy E cases are morally the same and if it is not wrong to help Nancy D then it isn't wrong to assist Nancy E. Finally, the only difference between the case of Nancy E and the case of Nancy F concerns where her lungs came from. Nancy E hasn't the lungs or "natural" ventilators she was born with; she has someone else's lungs. Nancy F has the lungs she was born with. If that makes no moral difference then the Nancy E and Nancy F cases are ethically equivalent. And if it is morally not wrong to help Nancy E die, it cannot be morally wrong to help Nancy F either.

The cases are morally indistinguisable

Of course, it is possible still to insist that it is morally unacceptable to help Nancy F die. But anyone who thinks this must also believe that it is improper to assist Nancy B. That's what the argument or reasoning, if it is sound, proves. The virtuous slippery slope argument establishes that the two cases are morally indistinguishable. What the argument or reasoning proves is that you cannot accept both that it is ethically acceptable to help Nancy B die but unacceptable to help Nancy F die.

Again, it is possible to insist that, even if these two cases are morally the same, this doesn't show that more generally, or always, active euthanasia is morally the same as passive euthanasia. This insistence is logically impeccable. On the other hand, the virtuous slippery slope argument presented here for the moral equivalence of the cases of Nancy B and Nancy F can obviously be mimicked for many other instances of active and passive euthanasia. The recipe is to start with either an instance of active or an instance of passive euthanasia, then to find or invent a similar case of the other, and then to construct appropriate intermediate cases, each case erasing a small factual difference which makes no moral difference. So, even though my argument only establishes the ethical equivalence of the Nancy B and Nancy F cases, it is easy to see how to establish that generally, for many different pairs of cases, or even always, active euthanasia is morally the same as passive euthanasia.

2

An Ethical Difference Exists Between Active and Passive Euthanasia

Michael Manning

Michael Manning is an associate pastor of St. Gregory the Great parish in Trenton, New Jersey. Manning practiced medicine as an internist and gastroenterologist for thirteen years before entering the seminary. He is the author of Euthanasia and Physician-Assisted Suicide: Killing or Caring? *from which the following viewpoint is excerpted.*

Professor of ethics Dan Maguire believes there is a moral difference between passive and active euthanasia, terms referred to as omission and commission. He believes passive and active euthanasia differ in their effects on family members as well as on doctors. For example, family members would feel more guilty if they administered fatal medication to a loved one than if they withheld antibiotics for pneumonia in a terminal case. Likewise, physicians would generally find it easier to stop supportive measures than to order a deadly injection for a patient. In cases of omission or passive euthanasia, assigning responsibility is not as clear-cut as in cases of commission or active euthanasia. Holding someone responsible for not doing something is more difficult than to hold someone responsible for a specific act.

Ethicist Dan Maguire discusses the omission/commission [passive/active euthanasia] problem with sensitivity and insight. What is the moral difference between killing and allowing to die? Is there guilt by omission? He tells the story of a woman who was legally convicted for failing to prevent the death by suicide of her husband, who hung himself before her in a fit of rage at the conclusion of an argument. She omitted the performance of any actions that would have saved his life. Most physicians would accept a distinction between failing to act medically and intervening directly to kill a patient. Even when the result is the same—death—it seems easier to justify omission rather than commission.

13

Some see no moral distinction between omission and commission regarding mercy killing. In their view, the distinction is a cloudy one, since the decision either to withhold medical treatment or to administer a fatal medication has the same result and, in fact, the same intention. "A decision not to keep a patient alive is as morally deliberate as a decision to end a life [as Maguire puts it]."

Differing effects

Simply because acts of omission and commission are both deliberate and have the same result does not confer moral equivalence, in Maguire's view. They differ in their effects. There is a difference to caregivers and family alike between failing to administer antibiotics for pneumonia in a terminal case and administering a fatal dose of morphine. Death, even when forestalled by appropriate and aggressive medical treatment, can bring on feelings of guilt in the survivors. The administration of a fatal medication would certainly compound their misgivings and guilt. A lingering and painful death, however, may also foster feelings of guilt for not having expedited death and helped to alleviate some of the suffering.

For almost all physicians, even those in favor of euthanasia, it would be easier to stop supportive or resuscitative measures than to administer or order a deadly injection.

For almost all physicians, even those in favor of euthanasia, it would be easier to stop supportive or resuscitative measures than to administer or order a deadly injection. Even if the cessation of medical treatment would bring about death as quickly as administration of a fatal drug, the physician who disconnects a respirator can feel as though he or she merely let the disease advance, or let death have its way. Maguire carefully notes that this does not mean that deliberate termination of a life could not be moral, only that most physicians would understand you if you said that omission and commission are not the same thing in cases of euthanasia.

Omission and commission also differ in their effects on society. The projected impact is greatest for those who subscribe to the "wedge theory," which holds that allowing any cases of euthanasia or assisted suicide could set off a chain reaction of unforeseen and disastrous consequences. But even those who justify certain cases of euthanasia must admit that death by commission gives more control to the one who dispenses the death, and might be abused for tax or inheritance purposes or for other ulterior motives.

Differ in deliberateness

Maguire notes that both actions may differ in their deliberateness. Omission may result from a kind of moral paralysis. It can be the result of the inability to overcome nonvolitional forces like the drag of moral acedia or confusion. While *not to decide* may also be *to decide*, it must also be admitted that sometimes it truly is "not to decide."

Omissions may, however, be fully deliberate and decisive acts. The decision not to operate on a child, for example, can be a painful decision reached after grave consideration. It is not, however, the same psychological act that moves you to give a child a fatal injection. Either act may be immoral or moral (according to Maguire), but they are not the same, and the distinctions may be crucial. The administration of a fatal dose of medication has a finality to it that failure to operate does not have. It closes off life and bars any other alternatives. For this reason, such a decision must be surrounded by even more serious deliberateness and moral analysis.

Moral agency is more diffuse in cases of omission. It is easier to say who did something than to say who did not do something. If what was omitted should have been done (at least in someone's view), then it is difficult to determine who is most responsible for the omission, since, literally, *everyone* did not do it.

Different forms

Finally, omission and commission take on different forms. Each can be specific and each may be moral or immoral, but not by virtue of belonging to a specific category. Maguire gives some examples of acts of omission: not steering a rolling car away from a child in its path; not stopping to tackle an armed robber; not giving insulin to an otherwise healthy diabetic; not giving morphine to a terminal cancer patient in pain; not attending to a terminal patient after all medication has been stopped. Each omission is different and needs to be subjected to ethical analysis and examination.

3

Suicide by the Terminally Ill Is Justified

Carol Bernstein Ferry

Carol Bernstein Ferry was a radical philanthropist who, with her first and second husbands, donated millions of dollars of inherited wealth to support leftist causes, including the Black Panthers, opposition to the Vietnam War, prison reform, and civil rights. Ferry also visited prisons and taught reading to inmates at Sing Sing prison in New York.

I have emphysema and tumors and have been given six months to a year to live. I believe that my final days will be filled with pain and distress not only for me but for my family. I've had a good life and feel it is my time to go and see no virtue in suffering. In light of these circumstances, I believe I am making a rational decision by choosing to end my life in a peaceful, painless, and acceptable way. It is regrettable that the legal system considers it a felony for anyone to help me commit suicide, and I hope that my letter will help make assisted suicide more acceptable for others. Making it illegal to help those we care about avoid suffering and attain a dignified death is a blot on our nation's character.

Editor's Note: Before she took her own life in June 2001, Carol Bernstein Ferry wrote the following open letter explaining her decision.

If my death can contribute to an understanding of euthanasia, then I want it to do so. That is why I am writing this letter, explaining why I choose to take active steps to end my life rather than waiting for death to come gradually. With this letter I also want to make it clear that, although I have the support and tacit agreement of my children and close friends, no one but myself will take the steps that cause death. It is unfortunate that I must say this; our laws are at a destructive point just now, so if anyone other than myself actually causes my death, that person will be liable to conviction as a felon. What an absurdity! To help someone facing a time—whether short or long—of pain and distress, whose death coming bit by bit can cause major sorrow and anxiety to family and

Carol Bernstein Ferry, "A Good Death," *Nation*, vol. 273, September 17, 2001, p. 8. Copyright © 2001 by The Nation Magazine/The Nation Company, Inc. Reproduced by permission.

friends, not to mention the medical help, quite useless, that must be expended in order to maintain a bearable level of pain—that this sensible deed can be construed a crime is a blot on our legal system and on our power of thought.

The idea that human life is sacred no matter the condition or the desire of the person seems to me irrational.

I have known since June [2000] that I am terminally ill. Emphysema, a tumor in my chest and recently a new tumor near my pelvis put it beyond question that I am on the way to death. This seems to me in no way a tragedy—I am, after all, 76 years old—but a natural ending. I don't feel called upon to suffer until the last minute of a creeping death, nor do I want to put my children through such a time, so I am choosing to make a finish while I am still able to function.

A life of joy

I've had a lucky life. I've had a lot of joy; I've had enough sorrow to know that I'm a member in good standing of the human race; I have tried to make myself useful. I have nothing to complain about, certainly not death. I feel lucky now, in that I have been given a somewhat definite span of life ahead. Once the approximate limit of that span—six months to a year from last June—got absorbed into my brain, many problems floated away. I no longer have to worry about death, as it is with me now. Every day is a treat, an extra gift, the positive side of the expression Borrowed Time. It is my hope that people close to me, especially my children, can also enjoy this relaxed attitude toward something that is, after all, inevitable. The idea that I can probably manage to have a peaceful and relatively painless ending is a comfort. For that probability to be a certainty would be the best comfort of all. But that certainty could only come if I were to have the help of a second person, and that I will not have, as under present law that person would be in immediate danger.

The moral beauty of suffering for its own sake is important to many, for reasons that I find unfathomable. Religious pressure, the idea that God enjoys our suffering, is beyond me. And the terrible attitude of our lawmakers and politicians, considering that any help toward a painless death should be punished, is a source of wonder and shame. A few states—notably Oregon and Maine—are trying to change their laws to allow the administration of pain killing medicine even if it hastens the moment of death. Even this moderate and humane act is being fought in legislatures of some states and in the Senate. The idea that human life is sacred no matter the condition or the desire of the person seems to me irrational.

Each person's life is his own

The people who think that it is immoral to make a rational decision about ending life certainly have the right to consider their own death in this light and to endure to the very end whatever pain awaits them and their families. But they have flowed over into the idea that it is their right also to control those others of us who view the matter differently. There are societies here and there that do not put up roadblocks when a person decides to end life. However, the idea that each person's life is his own is too radical or too abstruse for consumption in the United States. This is the attitude that I hope will change, and soon. It is the attitude that I hope to help soften by explaining that my suicide plan is bringing me and those close to me a measure of security that my life can end in as spirited a way as possible.

I appreciate everyone who has been involved in encouraging me, including those who have not encouraged me but who have withstood the temptation to reprimand me. My decision has been arrived at after many years of contemplation, not quickly or casually. I hope it will help others to feel all right about preferring a peaceful, benign path into death.

4

Suicide by the Terminally Ill Is Not Justified

Herbert Hendin

Herbert Hendin is a professor of psychiatry at the New York Medical College in Valhalla. He is also the medical director of the American Foundation for Suicide Prevention and author of Seduced by Death, *from which the following viewpoint was excerpted.*

The vast majority of those who request assisted suicide or euthanasia are having difficulty coping with the uncertainties of life, are dreading what will happen to them, and are feeling ambivalent about death. These patients are usually suffering from a treatable depressive condition that could be addressed with the help of a caring and knowledgeable physician. When the fears and anxieties which accompany depression are dealt with, and the patient can take care of unfinished business, requests for death usually cease. In fact, after treatment, the patient usually finds greater meaning and purpose in life. Instead of listening to the terminally ill patient's first fearful request for assisted suicide, the physician should help the patient deal with his or her feelings. Doctors should also be aware that any desire they have to help terminally ill patients die is merely their own attempt to control death and avoid feelings of inadequacy caused by their failure to cure the patient.

A few years ago, a young professional in his early thirties who had acute myelocytic leukemia was referred to me for consultation. With medical treatment, Tim was given a 25 percent chance of survival; without it, he was told, he would die in a few months. Tim, an ambitious executive whose focus on career success had led him to neglect his relationships with his wife and family, was stunned. His immediate reaction was a desperate, angry preoccupation with suicide and a request for support in carrying it out. He was worried about becoming dependent and feared both the symptoms of his disease and the side effects of treatment.

Tim's request speaks directly to the question at the heart of assisted suicide and euthanasia: Does our need to care for people who are terminally ill and to reduce their suffering require us to give physicians the right to end their lives?

Asking this question, however, helps make us aware that neither legalizing nor forbidding euthanasia addresses the much larger problem of providing humane care for those who are terminally ill. To some degree the call for legalization is a symptom of our failure to develop a better response to the problems of dying and the fear of unbearable pain or artificial prolongation of life in intolerable circumstances.

The desire for death waxes and wanes in terminally ill patients, even among those who express a persistent wish to die.

People are apt to assume that seriously or terminally ill people who wish to end their lives are different from those who are otherwise suicidal. Yet the first reaction of many patients, like Tim, to the knowledge of serious illness and possible death is anxiety, depression, and a wish to die. Such patients are not significantly different from patients who react to other crises with the desire to end the crisis by ending their lives.

Patients rarely cite the fear of death itself as their reason for requesting assisted suicide or euthanasia, but clinicians often see such patients displace anxieties about death onto the circumstances of dying: pain, dependence, loss of dignity, and the unpleasant side effects of medical treatments. Focusing one's fear or rage onto these palpable events distracts from the fear of death itself. Tim's anxieties about the painful circumstances that would surround his death were not irrational, but all his fears about dying amplified them.

Talking about death

Once Tim and I could talk about the possibility or likelihood of his dying—what separation from his family and the destruction of his body meant to him—his desperation subsided. He accepted medical treatment and used the remaining months of his life to become closer to his wife and parents. At first, he would not talk to his wife about his illness because of his resentment that she was going on with her life while he would likely not be going on with his. A session with the two of them cleared the air and made it possible for them to talk openly with each other. Two days before he died, Tim talked about what he would have missed without the opportunity for a loving parting.

The last days of most patients can be given such meaning if those treating them know how to engage them. Tim's need for communication with his wife, communication that was not possible until he voiced his envy and resentment over her going on with her life while he was probably not going to be doing so, finds parallels in the lives of most dying patients.

In a twist on conventional wisdom, the English palliative care specialist Robert Twycross has written, "where there is hope there is life," referring not to hope of a cure, but hope of doing something that gives meaning to life as long as it lasts. Virtually everyone who is dying has unfinished business, even if only the need to share their life and their death with friends, family, a doctor, or a hospice worker. Without such purpose, terminally ill patients who are not in great physical distress may be tortured by the feeling that they are only waiting to die and may want to die at once.

If assisted suicide were legal, Tim probably would have asked a doctor's help in taking his own life. Because he was mentally competent, he would have qualified for assisted suicide and would surely have found a doctor who would agree to his request.

Since the Oregon law and similar laws being considered in other states do not require an independently referred doctor for a second opinion, Tim would likely have been referred by a physician supportive of assisted suicide to a colleague who was equally supportive; the evaluation would have been pro forma. He could have been put to death in an unrecognized state of terror, unable to give himself the chance of getting well or of dying in the dignified way he did. The Oregon law is the latest example of how public frustration can lead to action that only compounds the problem; in the rush to legislate, advocates have failed to understand the problem they are claiming to solve.

Motivations for suicide

Long before today's movement to legalize assisted suicide of patients who are seriously or terminally ill, we knew that physical illness contributes significantly to the motivation for suicide. Medical illness plays an important role in 25 percent of suicides, and this percentage rises with age: from 50 percent in suicides who are over fifty years old, to over 70 percent in suicides older than sixty.

Most suicide attempts reflect a patient's ambivalence about dying, and those requesting assisted suicide show an equal ambivalence. The desire for death waxes and wanes in terminally ill patients, even among those who express a persistent wish to die. Some patients may voice suicidal thoughts in response to transient depression or severe pain, but these patients usually find relief with treatment of their depressive illness or pain and are grateful to be alive. Strikingly, the overwhelming majority of the patients who are terminally ill fight for life until the end; only 2 to 4 percent of suicides occur in the context of terminal illness.

The fact that a patient finds relief in the prospect of death is not a sign that the decision is appropriate.

Like Tim, the vast majority of those who request assisted suicide or euthanasia are motivated primarily by dread of what will happen to them rather than by current pain or suffering. Similarly, in several studies, more individuals, particularly elderly individuals, killed themselves because they feared or *mistakenly* believed they had cancer than killed themselves and actually had cancer. In the same way, preoccupation with suicide is greater in those awaiting the results of tests for HIV antibodies than in those who know that they are HIV positive.

Patients do not know what to expect and cannot foresee how their conditions will unfold as they decline toward death. Facing this ignorance, they fill the vacuum with their fantasies and fears. When these fears are dealt with by a caring and knowledgeable physician, the request for death usually disappears.

Mental illness contributes to suicide risk

Mental illness raises the suicide risk even more than physical illness. Nearly 95 percent of those who kill themselves have been shown to have a diagnosable psychiatric illness in the months preceding suicide. The majority suffer from depression that can be treated. This is particularly true of those over fifty, who are more prone than younger victims to take their lives during the type of acute depressive episode that responds most effectively to treatment.

Like other suicidal individuals, patients who desire an early death during a serious or terminal illness are usually suffering from a treatable depressive condition. Although pain and other factors such as lack of family support contribute to the wish for death, recent research has confirmed that none is as significant as the presence of depression, which researchers have found to be the only predictor of the desire for death.

Both patients who attempt suicide and those who request assisted suicide often test the affection and care of others, confiding feelings like "I don't want to be a burden to my family" or "My family would be better off without me." Such statements are classic indicators of suicidal depression.

Depression can be treated

Expressions of being a burden usually reflect depressed feelings of worthlessness or guilt, and may be pleas for reassurance. Whether physically healthy or terminally ill, these patients need assurance that they are still wanted; they also need treatment for depression. If the doctor does not recognize the ambivalence, anxiety, and depression that underlie a patient's request for death, the patient becomes trapped by that request and can die in a state of unrecognized terror.

In recent years we have become aware that in depressed patients anxiety, panic, or terror are symptoms that most strongly predict short-term risk for suicide. Desperation, which Tim exemplified in his initial interviews, best describes their affective state.

Unfortunately, depression itself is commonly underdiagnosed and often inadequately treated. Although most people who kill themselves are under medical care at the time of death, their physicians often fail to recognize the symptoms of depressive illness or, even if they do, fail to give adequate treatment.

The fact that a patient finds relief in the prospect of death is not a sign that the decision is appropriate. Patients who are depressed and suicidal may appear calm and less depressed after deciding to end their lives, whether by themselves or with the help of a doctor. It is coping with the uncertainties of life that agitate and depress them.

Depression, often precipitated by discovering one has a serious illness, also exaggerates the tendency toward seeing problems in black-or-white terms, overlooking solutions and alternative possibilities. Suicidal individuals are especially prone to put conditions on life: "I won't live without my husband," ". . . if I lose my looks, power, prestige, or health," or ". . . if I am to die soon." They are afflicted by the need to make demands on life that cannot be fulfilled. Determining the time, place, and circumstances of their death is the most dramatic expression of their need for control. When a patient finds a doctor who shares the view that life is worth living only if certain conditions are met, the patient's rigidity is reinforced.

An aspect of the depressed individual's need for control is the attempt to try to treat life as an intellectual balancing act. In drawing on the concept of *bilanz Selbstmord*, or "balanced suicide," promoted by German philosophers in the early part of this century, proponents of what is called "rational suicide" seem to be doing something similar. Balanced suicide is said to result when individuals assumed to be mentally unimpaired dispassionately took stock of their life situation, found it unacceptable, and foreseeing no significant change for the better, decided to end their lives.

Contemporary advocates see a close analogy between a rational decision for suicide and the decision of the directors of a firm to declare bankruptcy and go out of business. Yet the idea that life can be measured on a balance scale is itself a characteristic of suicidal people. Some of the most depressed suicidal patients spend years making elaborate lists of reasons why they should go on living to counter the many reasons they can think of for dying.

Doctors experience a sense of failure

Patients are not alone in their inability to tolerate situations they cannot control. Lewis Thomas has written insightfully about the sense of failure and helplessness that doctors may experience in the face of death; such feelings may explain why doctors have such difficulty discussing terminal illness with patients. A majority of doctors avoid such discussions, while most patients would prefer frank talk. These feelings might also explain both doctors' tendency to use excessive measures to maintain life and their need to make death a physician's decision. By deciding when patients die, by making death a medical decision, the physician preserves the illusion of mastery over the disease and the accompanying feelings of helplessness. The physician, not the illness, is responsible for the death. Assisting suicide and euthanasia become ways of dealing with the frustration of not being able to cure the disease.

5

Physician-Assisted Suicide Should Be Legalized

Peter Rogatz

Peter Rogatz is a physician who previously served as a professor of community and preventive medicine at the State University of New York at Stony Brook. He is also a founding board member of Compassion in Dying of New York, a member of the Ethics Committee of Hospice Care Network in Long Island and Queens, and a member of the Committee on Bioethical Issues of the Medical Society of the State of New York.

Physician-assisted suicide, a practice related to euthanasia, involves a physician providing medications or other means to a patient with the understanding that the patient intends to use them to commit suicide. Although opponents have many objections to this practice, and it is prohibited in every state except for Oregon, two principles outweigh all of their arguments: patient autonomy, or the individual's right to decide what to do with his or her own body, and the duty of the physician to relieve the patient's suffering. These principles support the legalization of physician-assisted suicide. Consequently, no laws should prohibit a physician from assisting a patient who is suffering from an incurable disease and who knowingly chooses to end his or her life. Rather than see physician-assisted suicide as "killing," opponents should see it as bringing the dying process to a merciful end.

Physician-assisted suicide is among the most hotly debated bioethical issues of our time. Every reasonable person prefers that no patient ever contemplate suicide—with or without assistance—and recent improvements in pain management have begun to reduce the number of patients seeking such assistance. However, there are some patients who experience terrible suffering that can't be relieved by any of the therapeutic or palliative techniques medicine and nursing have to offer, and some of those patients desperately seek deliverance.

Physician-assisted suicide isn't about physicians becoming killers. It's about patients whose suffering we can't relieve and about not turning away from them when they ask for help. Will there be physicians who feel they can't do this? Of course, and they shouldn't be obliged to. But if other physicians consider it merciful to help such patients by merely writing a prescription, it is unreasonable to place them in jeopardy of criminal prosecution, loss of license, or other penalty for doing so.

Many arguments are put forward for maintaining the prohibition against physician-assisted suicide, but I believe they are outweighed by two fundamental principles that support ending the prohibition: patient autonomy—the right to control one's own body—and the physician's duty to relieve suffering.

Physician-assisted suicide isn't about physicians becoming killers. It's about patients whose suffering we can't relieve and about not turning away from them when they ask for help.

Society recognizes the competent patient's right to autonomy—to decide what will or won't be done to his or her body. There is almost universal agreement that a competent adult has the right to self-determination, including the right to have life-sustaining treatment withheld or withdrawn. Suicide, once illegal throughout the United States, is no longer illegal in any part of the country. Yet assisting a person to take her or his own life is prohibited in every state but Oregon. If patients seek such help, it is cruel to leave them to fend for themselves, weighing options that are both traumatic and uncertain, when humane assistance could be made available.

The physician's obligations are many but, when cure is impossible and palliation has failed to achieve its objectives, there is always a residual obligation to relieve suffering. Ultimately, if the physician has exhausted all reasonable palliative measures, it is the patient—and only the patient—who can judge whether death is harmful or a good to be sought. Marcia Angell, former executive editor of the *New England Journal of Medicine*, has put it this way:

> The highest ethical imperative of doctors should be to provide care in whatever way best serves patients' interests, in accord with each patient's wishes, not with a theoretical commitment to preserve life no matter what the cost in suffering. . . . The greatest harm we can do is to consign a desperate patient to unbearable suffering—or force the patient to seek out a stranger like Dr. Kevorkian.

Arguments against physician-assisted suicide

Let's examine the key arguments made against physician-assisted suicide. First, much weight is placed on the Hippocratic injunction to do no harm. It has been asserted that sanctioning physician-assisted suicide "would give doctors a license to kill," and physicians who accede to such requests have been branded by some as murderers. This is both illogical and inflammatory. Withdrawal of life-sustaining treatment—for example, disconnecting a ventilator at a patient's request—is accepted by society, yet this requires a more definitive act by a physician than prescribing a medication that a patient has requested and is free to take or not, as he or she sees fit. Why should the latter be perceived as doing harm when the former is not? Rather than characterizing this as "killing," we should see it as bringing the dying process to a merciful end. The physician who complies with a plea for final release from a patient facing death under unbearable conditions is doing good, not harm, and her or his actions are entirely consonant with the Hippocratic tradition.

Second, it is argued that requests for assisted suicide come largely from patients who haven't received adequate pain control or who are clinically depressed and haven't been properly diagnosed or treated. There is no question that proper management of such conditions would significantly reduce the number of patients who consider suicide; any sanctioning of assistance should be contingent upon prior management of pain and depression.

A patient contemplating suicide would be much less likely to take such a step if he or she were confident of receiving assistance in the future if so desired.

However, treatable pain is not the only reason, or even the most common reason, why patients seek to end their lives. Severe body wasting, intractable vomiting, urinary and bowel incontinence, immobility, and total dependence are recognized as more important than pain in the desire for hastened death. There is a growing awareness that loss of dignity and of those attributes that we associate particularly with being human are the factors that most commonly reduce patients to a state of unrelieved misery and desperation.

Third, it is argued that permitting physician-assisted suicide would undermine the sense of trust that patients have in their doctors. This is curious reasoning; patients are not lying in bed wondering if their physicians are going to kill them—and permitting assisted suicide shouldn't create such fears, since the act of administering a fatal dose would be solely within the control of the patient. Rather than undermining a patient's trust, I would expect the legalization of physician-assisted suicide to enhance that trust. I have spoken with a great many people who feel that they would like to be able to trust their physicians to provide such help in the event of unrelieved suffering—and making that possible would give such patients a greater sense of security. Furthermore, some patients have taken their own lives at a relatively early stage of terminal illness precisely because they feared that progressively increasing disability, without anyone to assist them, would rob them of this option at a later time when they were truly desperate. A patient contemplating suicide would be much less likely to take such a step if he or she were confident of receiving assistance in the future if so desired.

Fourth, it is argued that patients don't need assistance to commit suicide; they can manage it all by themselves. This seems both callous and unrealistic. Are patients to shoot themselves, jump from a window, starve themselves to death, or rig a pipe to the car exhaust? All of these methods have been used by patients in the final stages of desperation, but it is a hideous experience for both patient and survivors. Even patients who can't contemplate such traumatic acts and instead manage to hoard a supply of lethal drugs may be too weak to complete the process without help and therefore face a high risk of failure, with dreadful consequences for themselves and their families.

Fifth, it is argued that requests for assisted suicide are not frequent enough to warrant changing the law. Interestingly, some physicians say they have rarely, if ever, received such requests, while others say they have often received requests. This is a curious discrepancy, but I think it can be explained: the patient who seeks help with suicide will cautiously test a physician's receptivity to the idea and simply won't approach a physician who is unreceptive. Thus, there are two subsets of physicians in this situation: those who are open to the idea of assisted suicide and those who aren't. Patients are likely to seek help from the former but not from the latter.

A study carried out a few years ago by the University of Washington School of Medicine queried 828 physicians (a 25 percent sample of primary care physicians and all physicians in selected medical sub specialties) with a response rate of 57 percent. Of these respondents, 12 percent reported receiving one or more explicit requests for assisted suicide, and one-fourth of the patients requesting such assistance received prescriptions.

A survey of physicians in San Francisco treating AIDS patients brought responses from half, and 53 percent of those respondents reported helping patients take their own lives by prescribing lethal doses of narcotics. Clearly, requests for assisted suicide can't be dismissed as rare occurrences.

Protections can be put in place that will minimize the risk of abuse.

Sixth, it is argued that sanctioning assisted suicide would fail to address the needs of patients who are incompetent. This is obviously true, since proposals for legalization specify that assistance be given only to a patient who is competent and who requests it. However, in essence, this argument says that, because we can't establish a procedure that will deal" with every patient, we won't make assisted suicide available to any patient. What logic! Imagine the outcry if that logic were applied to a procedure such as organ transplantation, which has benefited so many people in this country.

Seventh, it is argued that once we open the door to physician-assisted suicide we will find ourselves on a slippery slope leading to coercion and involuntary euthanasia of vulnerable patients. Why so? We have learned to grapple with many slippery slopes in medicine—such as Do Not Resuscitate (DNR) orders and the withdrawal of life support. We don't deal with those slippery slopes by prohibition but, rather, by adopting reasonable ground rules and setting appropriate limits.

The slippery slope argument discounts the real harm of failing to respond to the pleas of real people and considers only the potential harm that might be done to others at some future time and place. As in the case of other slippery slopes, theoretical future harm can be mitigated by establishing appropriate criteria that would have to be met before a patient could receive assistance. Such criteria have been outlined frequently. Stated briefly, they include:

1. The patient must have an incurable condition causing severe, unrelenting suffering.
2. The patient must understand his or her condition and prognosis, which must be verified by an independent second opinion.
3. All reasonable palliative measures must have been presented to and considered by the patient.
4. The patient must clearly and repeatedly request assistance in dying.
5. A psychiatric consultation must be held to establish if the patient is suffering from a treatable depression.
6. The prescribing physician, absent a close preexisting relationship (which would be ideal), must get to know the patient well enough to understand the reasons for her or his request.
7. No physician should be expected to violate his or her own basic values. A physician who is unwilling to assist the patient should facilitate transfer to another physician who would be prepared to do so.
8. All of the foregoing must be clearly documented.

Application of the above criteria would substantially reduce the risk of abuse but couldn't guarantee that abuse would never occur. We must recognize, however, that abuses occur today—in part because we tolerate covert action that is subject to no safeguards at all. A more open process would, in the words of philosopher and ethicist Margaret Battin, "prod us to develop much stronger protections for the kinds of choices about death we already make in what are often quite casual, cavalier ways."

It seems improbable that assisted suicide would pose a special danger to the elderly, infirm, and disabled. To paraphrase [economist] John Maynard Keynes, in the long run we are all elderly, infirm, or disabled and, since society well knows this, serious attention would surely be given to adequate protections against abuse. It isn't my intention to dispose glibly of the fear that society would view vulnerable patients as a liability and would manipulate them to end their lives prematurely. Of course, this concern must be respected, but the risk can be minimized by applying the criteria listed above. Furthermore, this argument assumes that termination of life is invariably an evil against which we must protect vulnerable patients who are poor or otherwise lacking in societal support. But, by definition, we are speaking of patients who desperately wish final release from unrelieved suffering, and poor and vulnerable patients are least able to secure aid in dying if they want it. The well-to-do patient may, with some effort and some good luck, find a physician who is willing to provide covert help; the poor and disenfranchised rarely have access to such assistance in today's world.

Eighth, it is argued that the Netherlands experience proves that societal tolerance of physician-assisted suicide leads to serious abuse. Aside from the fact that the data are subject to varying interpretation depending upon which analysis one believes, the situation in the Netherlands holds few lessons for us, because for many years that country followed the ambiguous practice of technically prohibiting but tacitly permitting assisted suicide and euthanasia.

The climate in the United States is different; our regulatory mechanisms would be different—much stricter, of course—and we should expect different outcomes. The experience of Oregon—the only one of our fifty states to permit physician-assisted suicide—is instructive. During the first three years that Oregon's law has been in effect, seventy terminally ill patients took advantage of the opportunity to self-administer medication to end protracted dying. Despite dire warnings, there was no precipitous rush by Oregonians to embrace assisted suicide. The poor and the uninsured weren't victimized; almost all of these seventy patients had health insurance, most were on hospice care, and most were people with at least some college education. There were no untoward complications. The Oregon experience is far more relevant for the United States than the Dutch experience, and it vindicates those who, despite extremely vocal opposition, advocated for the legislation.

Ninth, it has been argued that a society that doesn't assure all its citizens the right to basic health care and protect them against catastrophic health costs has no business considering physician-assisted suicide. I find this an astonishing argument. It says to every patient who seeks ultimate relief from severe suffering that his or her case won't be considered until all of us are assured basic health care and financial protection. These are certainly proper goals for any decent society, but they won't be attained in the United States until it becomes a more generous and responsible nation—and that day seems to be far off. Patients seeking deliverance from unrelieved suffering shouldn't be held hostage pending hoped-for future developments that are not even visible on the distant horizon.

Finally, it is argued that the status quo is acceptable—that a patient who is determined to end his or her life can find a sympathetic physician who will provide the necessary prescription and that physicians are virtually never prosecuted for such acts. There are at least four reasons to reject the status quo. First, it forces patients and physicians to undertake a clandestine conspiracy to violate the law, thus compromising the integrity of patient, physician, and family. Second, such secret compacts, by their very nature, are subject to faulty implementation with a high risk of failure and consequent tragedy for both patient and family. Third, the assumption that a determined patient can find a sympathetic physician applies, at best, to middle- and upper-income persons who have ongoing relationships with their physicians; the poor, as I've already noted, rarely have such an opportunity. Fourth, covert action places a physician in danger of criminal prosecution or loss of license and, although such penalties are assumed to be unlikely, that risk certainly inhibits some physicians from doing what they believe is proper to help their patients.

Reducing the incentive for suicide

I believe that removing the prohibition against physician assistance, rather than opening the flood gates to ill-advised suicides, is likely to reduce the incentive for suicide: patients who fear great suffering in the final stages of illness would have the assurance that help would be available if needed and they would be more inclined to test their own abilities to withstand the trials that lie ahead.

Life is the most precious gift of all, and no sane person wants to part with it, but there are some circumstances where life has lost its value. A competent person who has thoughtfully considered his or her own situation and finds that unrelieved suffering outweighs the value of continued life shouldn't have to starve to death or find other drastic and violent solutions when more merciful means exist. Those physicians who wish to fulfill what they perceive to be their humane responsibilities to their patients shouldn't be forced by legislative prohibition into covert actions.

There is no risk-free solution to these very sensitive problems. However, I believe that reasonable protections can be put in place that will minimize the risk of abuse and that the humanitarian benefits of legalizing physician-assisted suicide outweigh that risk. All physicians are bound by the injunction to do no harm, but we must recognize that harm may result not only from the commission of a wrongful act but also from the omission of an act of mercy. While not every physician will feel comfortable offering help in these tragic situations, many believe it is right to do so and our society should not criminalize such humanitarian acts.

6

Physicians Should Never Participate in Euthanasia

Leon R. Kass

Leon R. Kass is the chairman of the President's Council on Bioethics. He is a researcher in molecular biology, bioethics, ethics, philosophy, family, and social mores. Kass is also a former surgeon and a professor at the College and the Committee on Social Thought at the University of Chicago. Among the books Kass has written are The Ethics of Human Cloning *and* Life, Liberty, and the Defense of Dignity: The Challenge of Bioethics.

The medical profession has an intrinsic moral character which prohibits its members from practicing euthanasia. Traditional professional ethics demand that the physician devote him or herself to healing the sick and to serving the higher good of health and wholeness. In support of these ethics, the physician is required to embrace certain virtues, including moderation, self-restraint, sympathy, truthfulness, and encouragement. Accompanying these virtues is the unchangeable rule that doctors must not kill; ending a patient's life is not compatible with the true values of the medical profession.

That we die is certain. When and how we die is not. Because we want to live and not to die, we resort to medicine to delay the inevitable. Yet in some cases, medicine's success in preserving life has been purchased at a heavy price, paid in the coin of *how* we die: often in conditions of great pain and suffering, irreversible incompetence, and terminal loss of control. In these circumstances, many Americans increasingly seek greater control over the end of life, and some even wish to elect death to avoid the burdens of lingering on. Ironically, they also seek assistance in doing so from the death-defying art of medicine. People no longer talk only about refusing medical treatment. The demands of the day are for physician-assisted suicide and euthanasia. Voters in the state of Oregon have legalized physician-assisted suicide; a large segment of national public opinion approves the practice of doctor-induced death; and even many physicians ap-

Leon R. Kass, "'I Will Give No Deadly Drug': Why Doctors Must Not Kill," *The Case Against Assisted Suicide*, edited by Kathleen Foley and Herbert Hendin. Baltimore: Johns Hopkins University Press, 2002. Copyright © 2002 by The Johns Hopkins University Press. Reproduced by permission.

pear ready to overturn the centuries-old taboo against medical killing. Euthanasia practiced by physicians seems to be an idea whose time has come.

But in my view, it remains a bad idea whose time must not come—not now, not ever. Powerful reasons, of both prudence and principle, have for centuries supported such a judgment, and, as I will argue, they do so still, despite our changed circumstances—indeed, all the more so because of them. The heart of the argument rests on understanding the special moral character of the medical profession and the ethical obligations that it entails. Accordingly, I will be considering these interrelated questions: What are the norms that all physicians, *as physicians*, should agree to observe, whatever their personal opinions and private morality? What is the basis of such a medical ethic? What does it say—and what should we think—about doctors intentionally killing?

Contemporary ethical approaches

The question about physicians killing appears, at first glance, to be just a special case of this general question: May or ought one kill people who ask to be killed? Those who answer this general question in the affirmative offer two reasons. First is freedom or autonomy: Each person has a right to control his or her body and his or her life, including the end of it. Some go as far as to assert a right to die, a strange claim in a liberal society founded on the need to secure and defend the inalienable right to life. But strange or not, for patients too weak to oppose potent life-prolonging technologies wielded by aggressive physicians, the claim based on choice, autonomy, and self-determination is certainly understandable. In this view, physicians (or others) are bound to acquiesce in demands not only for termination of treatment but also for intentional killing through poison, because the right to choose—freedom—must be respected, even more than life itself, and even when the physician would never recommend or concur with the choices made. Physicians, as keepers of the vials of life and death, are morally bound actively to dispatch the embodied person out of deference to autonomous personal choice.

The heart of the argument rests on understanding the special moral character of the medical profession and the ethical obligations that it entails.

The second reason for killing the patient who asks for death has little to do with choice. Instead, death is to be directly and swiftly given because the patient's life is deemed no longer worth living, according to some substantive or "objective" measure. Unusually great pain or a terminal condition or an irreversible coma or advanced senility or extreme degradation is the disqualifying quality of life that pleads—choice or no choice—for merciful termination. Choice may enter indirectly to confirm the judgment: if the patient does not speak up, the doctor (or a relative or some other proxy) may be asked to affirm that he would not himself choose—or that his patient, were he able to choose, would not choose—to remain alive with one or more of these stigmata. It is not his autonomy but rather the miserable and pitiable condition of his body or mind that justifies doing the patient in. Absent such substantial degradations, requests for assisted death would not be honored. Here the body itself offends and must be plucked out, from compassion or mercy, to be sure. Not the autonomous will of the patient, but the doctor's benevolent and compassionate love for suffering humanity justifies the humane act of mercy killing.

These two reasons advanced to justify the killing of patients correspond to the two approaches to medical ethics most prominent in the field today: the school of autonomy and the school of general benevolence and compassion (or love). Despite their differences, they are united in their opposition to the belief that medicine is intrinsically a moral profession, with *its own* immanent principles and standards of conduct that set limits on what physicians may properly do. Each seeks to remedy the ethical defect of a profession seen to be in itself *a*moral, technically competent but morally neutral.

Being a professional is . . . more than being a technician. It is rooted in our moral nature.

For the first ethical school, morally neutral technique is morally used only when it is used according to the wishes of the patient as client or consumer. The model of the doctor-patient relationship is one of contract: the physician—a highly competent hired syringe, as it were—sells his services on demand, restrained only by the law. Here's the deal: for the patient, autonomy and service; for the doctor, money, graced by the pleasure of giving the patient what he wants. If a patient wants to fix his nose or change his gender, determine the sex of unborn children, or take euphoriant drugs just for kicks, the physician can and will go to work—provided that the price is right.

For the second ethical school, morally neutral technique is morally used only when it is used under the guidance of general benevolence or loving charity. Not the will of the patient, but the humane and compassionate motive of the physician—not as physician but as human being—makes the doctor's actions ethical. Here, too, there can be strange requests and even stranger deeds, but if they are done from love, nothing can be wrong—again, providing the law is silent. All acts—including killing the patient—done lovingly are licit, even praiseworthy. Good and humane intentions can sanctify any deed.

In my opinion, both of these approaches misunderstand the moral foundations of medical practice and therefore provide an inadequate basis for medical ethics. For one thing, neither of them can make sense of some specific duties and restraints long thought absolutely inviolable under the traditional medical ethic (e.g., the proscription against having sex with patients). Must we now say that sex with a patient is permissible if the patient wants it and the price is right, or, alternatively, if the doctor is gentle and loving and has a good bedside manner? Or do we glimpse in this absolute prohibition a deeper understanding of the medical vocation, which the prohibition both embodies and protects? Indeed, as I will now try to show, the medical profession has its own intrinsic ethic, which a physician true to the calling will not violate, either for love or for money.

Profession: Intrinsically ethical

Let me propose a different way of thinking about medicine as a profession. Consider medicine not as a mixed marriage between its own value-neutral technique and some extrinsic moral principles, but as an inherently ethical activity, in which technique and conduct are both ordered in relation to an overarching good, the naturally given end of health. This once-traditional view of medicine I have defended at length in my book *Toward a More Natural Science*. Here I will present the conclusions without the arguments. It will suffice, for present purposes, if I can render this view plausible.

A profession, as etymology suggests, is an activity or occupation to which its practitioner publicly professes—that is, confesses—devotion. Learning may, of course, be required of, and prestige may, of course, be granted to, the professional, but it is the profession's goal that calls, that learning serves, and that prestige honors. Each of the ways of life to which the various professionals profess their devotion must be a way of life worthy of such devotion—and so they all are. The teacher devotes himself to helping people learn, looking up to truth and wisdom; the lawyer (or judge) devotes himself to rectifying injustice for his client (or for the parties before the court), looking up to what is lawful and right; the clergyman devotes himself to tending the souls of his parishioners, looking up to the sacred and the divine; and the physician devotes himself to healing the sick, looking up to health and wholeness.

Being a professional is thus more than being a technician. It is rooted in our moral nature; it is a matter not only of the mind and hand but also of the heart, not only of intellect and skill but also of character. For it is only as a being willing and able to devote himself to others and to serve some high good that a person makes a public profession of his way of life. To profess is an ethical act, and it makes the professional qua professional a moral being who prospectively affirms the moral nature of his activity.

Professing oneself a professional is an ethical act for many reasons. It is an articulate public act, not merely a private and silent choice—a confession before others who are one's witnesses. It freely promises continuing devotion, not merely announces present preferences, to a way of life, not just a way to a livelihood, a life of action, not only of thought. It serves some high good, which calls forth devotion because it is both good and high, but which requires such devotion because its service is most demanding and difficult, and thereby engages one's character, not merely one's mind and hands.

The good to which the medical profession is chiefly devoted is health, a naturally given although precarious standard or norm, characterized by "wholeness" and "well-working," toward which the living body moves on its own. Even the modern physician, despite great technological prowess, is finally but an assistant to natural powers of self-healing. As the healing profession, medicine uses artful means to serve the human body's natural efforts to maintain its integrity and its native powers and activities.

But health, though a goal tacitly sought and explicitly desired, is difficult to attain and preserve. It can be ours only provisionally and temporarily, for we are finite and frail. Medicine thus finds itself in between: the physician is called to serve the high and universal goal of health while also ministering to the needs and relieving the sufferings of the frail and particular patient. Moreover, the physician must respond not only to illness but also to its meaning for each individual, who, in addition to symptoms, may suffer from self-concern—and often fear and shame—about weakness and vulnerability, neediness and dependence, loss of self-esteem, and the fragility of all that matters to him. Thus the inner meaning of the art of medicine is derived from the pursuit of health and the care for the ill and suffering, guided by the self-conscious awareness, shared (even if only tacitly) by physician and patient alike, of the delicate and dialectical tension between wholeness and necessary decay.

When the activity of healing the sick is thus understood, we can discern certain virtues requisite for practicing medicine—among them, moderation and self-restraint, gravity, patience, sympathy, discretion, and prudence. We can also discern specific positive duties, addressed mainly to the patient's vulnerability and self-concern—including the demands for truthfulness, patient instruction, and encouragement. And, arguably, we can infer the importance of certain negative duties, formulable as absolute and unexceptionable rules. Among these, I submit, is this rule: Doctors must not kill. . . .

I am not arguing here against euthanasia per se. More importantly, I am not arguing against the cessation of medical treatment when such treatment merely prolongs painful or degraded dying; nor do I oppose the use of certain measures to relieve suffering that have, as an unavoidable consequence, an increased risk of death. Doctors may and must allow to die, even if they must not intentionally kill.

7

Withdrawing Life Support from the Terminally Ill Is Ethically Acceptable

Agata A. Bednarz

Agata A. Bednarz is a medical student at the University of Rochester in New York.

It is ultimately respect for the autonomy of the terminally ill patients that makes it ethically acceptable to withdraw life support from them. Having endured long months of pain and suffering with no hope of relief, these patients should have the physician's support when choosing to end their lives. Physicians who insist on keeping such patients alive are breaching the principle of non-maleficence (doing no harm). In addition to being ethical, the removal of life-sustaining treatment is not considered an act of physician-assisted suicide and thus is perfectly legal. The refusal of treatment is not a privilege but a right of the terminally ill.

Through the cobwebs of childhood memory, I can still remember the strange smell that hit my nostrils when I opened the front door of my home in Poland, curious to see whether the new day had brought any change to my grandmother's state of health. Earlier full of wit and life, she was now fading away with renal failure and other complications, as well as a consciousness swollen with hatred toward her quality of life and guilt that she was a burden to us. As I entered the dining room, the scent got stronger and the image of my grandmother spread comfortably on the couch struck me with a realization of what had happened.

Despite my views now, the first impulse of my eight-year-old self, other than opening all windows, was to dial the Polish equivalent of 911 and Mom's work number. This should have been the end to my grandmother's suffering but, despite her comatose state and my mother's pleas to take her off life-support, she awakened again, after three weeks in a coma, only to face another six long months of unbearable suffering. Why did the physicians insist on keeping her on life-support despite their

Agata A. Bednarz, "Death with Dignity: Withdrawal of Life Support," *The Humanist*, vol. 60, May/ June 2000, pp. 28–30. Copyright © 2000 by the American Humanist Association. Reproduced by permission.

knowledge of her well-thought-out opinions, this obvious "quitting" attempt, and the requests of my mother (who was her health care proxy) to end her suffering? I cannot vouch for the personal philosophy of the physicians who took care of Grandma. Nor can I bear witness to their training and ethical framework. Nonetheless, I would like to explore the issue of the withdrawal of life-support as it stands now, after sixteen years of heated debate.

Modern ethical dilemmas

With the advancement of humankind via medicine and technology that combat the natural course of action come the ethical dilemmas intrinsic to anything that is not of supernatural origin. These are especially evident in the arena of terminally ill patients or those who wish to die. The request for withdrawal of life-sustaining treatment put forth by the family, as in Grandma's case, burdens physicians with fear that they would be committing an illegal act of physician-assisted suicide by doing so. Physicians may be concerned about the violation of the principles of beneficence [to do good] and nonmaleficence [to do no harm] sworn to in the Hippocratic oath, as well as the damage to the integrity of medicine as a healing art that might ensue from such an act. In my opinion, in addition to these concerns, the more modern ethical issues at stake here could be the principle of patient autonomy and the idea of the quality of life as chosen and perceived by the patient—both key components in the patient-physician relationship.

In view of my medical training and current personal opinion, had I been on an ethical committee (granting there ever was one) advising the physician on this issue, I would—respecting my grandmother's autonomy as expressed by the substituted judgment of her surrogate agent and consistent with the principle of nonmaleficence—recommend that her life-support be disconnected and she be allowed to die in her own house, according to her wishes and life values. Not doing so would be a violation of her autonomy and would, as it had done, subject her to long months of pain and suffering that would breach the principles of nonmaleficence. The course of action the physicians chose to take was quite alienated from the wishes my grandmother had expressed throughout her years of treatment.

It must be said, however, that sixteen years ago, in a paternalistic communist country that Poland was, the doctor-patient relationship had a very different premise: one of authoritarian physician and submissive patient. To add to that, the strength and prevalence of the Roman Catholic church was the driving factor for many of the medical decisions made at that time and does not so strongly apply to the current situation in the United States.

Killing versus letting die

The rationale behind foregoing life-sustaining treatment as not an act of killing is a multifaceted one. First of all, it needs to be stressed that the causative agent for the fatality is the disease already present. Technology is controversial in that it equips us to prevent the natural course of action in terms of disease, yet in many cases it has the negative effect of delaying the inevitable death and prolonging suffering. It is indeed true that physician-assisted suicide is currently illegal in order to prevent a slippery-slope situation [a situation in which euthanasia becomes immorally used]. However, as established by courts, the removal of life-sustaining treatment is not legally considered an act of physician-assisted suicide. In addition, as it has been shown in the case of Dr. Timothy Quill,[1] in some cases sufficient moral reasons exist to justify physician-assisted suicide.

The autonomy, value of life, and suffering of patients have to be considered and regarded on an individual basis.

The deliberation about "killing versus letting die" has an additional interesting twist in the comparison of the evil of taking human life to the perception of what this life means to the individual and how that affects the degree of this misdeed. The general attitude about taking a life is that it causes the loss of one's capacity to plan and choose a future and deprives one of life's goods and joys. One reason why many physicians object to the withdrawal of life-sustaining treatment is that they see it as an active action of this evil—an action that might not be in agreement with their medical integrity or religious beliefs. As I mentioned above, the fact that my grandmother's physicians were Catholic most likely had some bearing on their decision. Nevertheless, we need not forget that she had suffered increasingly from her disease and advancing age and had decided there was not much left to live for. It is an autonomous perception that she had upheld for a long time and as a competent adult had a right to make. This sort of decision should be sacred to a physician, regardless of how it may interfere with the Hippocratic oath.

Naturally, some would argue against such a decision based on the view of the sanctity of life: that is, everyone, not only physicians, has an essential task to preserve life; therefore ending life is not justifiable under any circumstances. The problem with using the sanctity of life as an argument is that, as it turns out, it is not always an absolute. There are instances when taking a life, especially one's own (in defense of certain beliefs or as a sacrifice for loved ones), is accepted even by the strongest believers in the concept. Is life of infinite value then? It would appear that life itself doesn't present any value; rather, it serves as a vehicle for realizing other values—the basic gear in the human quest for fulfilling goals and desires.

One would have to agree then that, in my grandmother's case, as evidenced by her suicide attempt, life no longer held major values and no longer served as a vehicle for realizing those values. Consequently, even though I agree that the sanctity of life view is an important concept to prevent the slippery-slope phenomenon, it is my belief that the autonomy, value of life, and suffering of patients have to be considered and regarded on an individual basis.

---

1. Timothy Quill is a professor of medicine and psychiatry at the University of Rochester in New York who wrote a groundbreaking article on how he assisted one of his patients in committing suicide.

Withdrawing life-support

The remaining issue is the perceived legal implications of withdrawing life-sustaining medical treatment. Although many believe it to be an action of physician-assisted suicide, in reality withdrawing life-support has been affirmed in court many times (*Quinlan, Herbert, Linares,* and the like). If certain conditions are fulfilled, it is a procedure in which the physician (or health care proxy) is acting within the limits of the law. The conditions required are the following:

- It is virtually certain that further medical intervention will not attain any of the goals of medicine other than sustaining organic life.
- The preferences of the patient are not known and cannot be expressed.
- The quality of life clearly falls below minimal.
- Family and members of the staff are in accord.

The first condition was fulfilled in my grandmother's case, for the physicians gave no hope of her recovery. Additionally, based on the 1984 California Appellate Court ruling in *Bartling v. Superior Court,* I would argue that this condition is not necessary to make the refusal of treatment honored within the legal limit. As shown in *Bartling,* the ethicists and courts primarily consider the patient's autonomous choice or, if that's not available, the substituted judgment of the health care proxy or family.

Refusal of treatment is not a privilege *of terminally ill patients but, rather, a* right *that all patients have and is accordingly respected in the courts.*

The second condition—the issue of capacity—is often an object of controversy, as it is very difficult to determine in terminally ill patients. One of the prerequisites for deciding capacity is the ability to make and communicate one's preferences. In the case of my grandmother, it was obvious to the family that she had always retained the awareness of her situation. Her drive toward choosing death was quite understandable to us, considering her remarks on her current quality of life. Regardless of that, if the case were such that she was fully lacking the capacity to make a decision about her medical treatment, we are under the obligation to respect the substituted judgment of her health care proxy. Once again, this is based on the ethical principle that the autonomy of a competent patient should be the prevailing factor in all decision-making processes in a medical setting.

Determining the quality of life

The third point in the set of criteria for legal withdrawal of medical treatment is a controversial one because quality of life is a value judgment that might be subjective and often divergent between physicians and patients. The search for objective criteria is a question of great complexity that would require a philosophical debate. However, several conditions were determined in 1992 under which most people, were they able to choose, would prefer death. It is generally agreed that *minimal* quality of life can be described as a condition that has deteriorated beyond recovery and under which the patient appears to suffer discomfort or pain. The quality of life descends *below minimal* when the patient suffers extreme debilitation as well as complete and irreversible loss of sensory and intellectual ability (for example, patients on opiates for pain).

In my grandmother's case, it could be argued that, given her diagnosis of terminal renal failure with other complications and advanced age, her quality of life was minimal or below. This can be further supported by her understanding that her life no longer carried a quality she had learned to expect from it, which ultimately led her to the act of trying to end it.

As was already mentioned, the fourth condition of family agreement was fulfilled, and the staff disagreement stemming from legal concerns would nowadays be expected to change with the reassurance that withholding or withdrawing treatment are both legal procedures.

Ethical decision making

In conclusion, I would like to underline several concepts that I see as most important in the ethical decisions regarding terminally ill individuals. Refusal of treatment is controversial in terms of the physician's principle of beneficence. Perhaps a way to avoid this dilemma, however, would be to develop a list of conditions (age, life expectancy with and without treatment, the level of incapacity with and without treatment, the degree of pain and suffering, and so forth) that would be used to determine whether the right to refuse treatment should be respected. The flaw with this view is that the focus shifts to the patient's physical condition rather than her or his choice. This ultimately leads to decision making *about* the patient instead of *by* the patient, thus violating the most salient feature of modern ethics and the physician-patient relationship: the patient's autonomy.

Since I have already described the role of autonomy in medical decision making, I want to stress a fact that is often forgotten: refusal of treatment is not a *privilege* of terminally ill patients but, rather, a *right* that all patients have and is accordingly respected in the courts. The decision of burdens-versus-benefits as they are reflected in the patient's quality of life is one that can only be made by the patient in compliance with his or her values. This has even been recognized by presidential commission: "Quality of life is an ethically essential concept that focuses on the good of an individual . . . whether [his or her] condition will allow the individual to have a life that he/she views as worth living." It is my main recommendation that these words be taken deeply into consideration by both physicians and families involved in making decisions about the lives of patients. In modern "democratic" medicine, the physicians are there to serve and advise, and only in extreme situations of incapacity, emergency, lack of available health care proxy, or patient's waiver of decision making can they decide for a patient.

8

Religions Sometimes Approve of Euthanasia

Courtney S. Campbell

Courtney S. Campbell is a professor of philosophy at Oregon State University in Corvallis. Campbell is also the director of the Program for Ethics, Science, and the Environment at the university.

Religious traditions and values can offer guidance to people facing difficult decisions about whether to discontinue medical treatment or request physician-assisted suicide. Major religions usually oppose suicide but exceptions are made. For example, some Western religions hold that the purpose of life is the development of a "religious self"; if the dignity of the individual cannot be preserved, the preservation of life is not seen as an absolute good. Similarly, in the Eastern religions of Hinduism and Buddhism, a patient can shorten his or her life if the act is performed out of compassion for others, such as family members caring for the dying patient. Because both Hinduism and Buddhism see the goal of life as the liberation of the individual from materialism, euthanasia or "mercy killing" could be viewed as acceptable if the dying individual was in physical pain and striving for liberation.

In "The Parable of the Mustard Seed", the Buddha teaches a lesson that is valid for all cultures: human beings receive no exemption from mortality. Deep in the throes of grief after the death of her son, a woman seeks wisdom from the Buddha, who says that he does indeed have an answer to her queries. Before giving it, however, he insists that she must first collect a grain of mustard seed from every house that has not been touched by death. She canvasses her entire community, but fails to collect a single seed. Returning to the Buddha, she understands that, like all other living beings, we are destined to die.

Death is a defining characteristic of human experience. Yet, while the event of death remains elusively beyond human control, the process of dying has increasingly been brought into the domain of medicine and life-extending technologies. Some technologies, including organ trans-

Courtney S. Campbell, "Euthanasia and Religion," *UNESCO Courier*, vol. 53, January 2000, p. 37.

plantation, respirators, antibiotics like penicillin, and feeding tubes, enable life to be prolonged. Other technologies may hasten death.

The decision to use these technologies is a moral choice, because it involves a decision about a fundamental human good, the preservation of life. Yet, in some situations, a resort to technology to stave off death comes at a price of compromising another fundamental human value, the quality of that life. Decisions about continuing treatment for the dying or of allowing death to take place by foregoing or terminating such treatment, or even by physician-assisted suicide or euthanasia are thus both existentially and ethically agonizing. As individuals and their families face these controversial questions and as many countries consider revising their laws on end-of-life choices, religious traditions and values can offer guidance and insight, if not solutions.

Much religious opposition is based on concern for patients who may be in vulnerable positions because of their illness or their lack of social and economic resources.

Historically, religious communities have sought to appropriate death within the life cycle through rituals of remembrance, and religious teachings have emphasized that death brings meaning to mortality. The process of dying is often portrayed as an invitation to spiritual insight and a key moment in the cultivation of spiritual identity.

The world's great traditions of moral wisdom all begin with a strong predisposition to favour the preservation of life, although the specific reasons for this conviction vary from tradition to tradition. Turning first to three monotheistic religious traditions which have had global influence, Judaism, Christianity and Islam, for all their differences, basically address ethical issues concerning the end of life from a common value perspective. In particular, discussions centre on the values of sovereignty, stewardship, and the self.

Sovereignty denotes that the lives and bodies of persons are created by, and ultimately return to, God. We owe our existence to a loving Being who has graciously brought us into being. Thus, the fundamental passages in human life, including birth and death, are of divine concern. This understanding of sovereignty has significant implications for decision-making at the end of life. It bestows sacredness upon human life, which supports the impulse towards preserving life by available medical technologies. Yet sovereignty also entails that the ultimate authority for deciding our mortal passages belongs to God. Human beings must not overstep these boundaries, or so to speak "play God" with life and death.

"Agents of God"

Through the value of stewardship, we are considered "agents of God", called to carry out the work of divine intent on earth. This task entails decision-making responsibilities for which we are accountable: our actions either further or violate divine intent. In addition, as emphasized in

Islamic teaching, we are the trustees or stewards of our bodies. We are therefore entrusted with the capacities and responsibility to make appropriate decisions when confronting a treatment choice at the end of our own life or that of a loved one.

Indeed, with very few exceptions, the major faith traditions of the West have rejected a view known as "vitalism", which holds that biological life is to be preserved at all costs and with all available technologies. Vitalism is considered theologically mistaken because it appears to make divine will and intent contingent upon the state of medical technology. In other words, it puts technology in the role of God.

The dignity of persons, linked to the notion of "self", is another core value of these monotheistic faith traditions. In Jewish and Christian thought, this is expressed in the idea that humans are distinctively in the "image of God". Islamic theology does not use such language, but no less affirms the significant value of persons. The "religious self" is constituted in part by the person's rationality, freedom, and decision-making capacity, but also by relationships (with loved ones, for example) and bodily integrity. These characteristics support human responsibility in addressing end of life decisions, including refusals of medical procedures that invade the body with no real benefit, in the context of a caring community. Put another way, preserving life is not an absolute good in and of itself. Life is a good that opens the way to achieving higher goods that constitute the religious self.

Foregoing life support

So by looking within the moral parameters set by these three values of sovereignty, stewardship, and the self, we find that a patient can decide to forego life support. A doctor can also allow a patient to die if the continuation of life (by technological means) assaults the dignity of the person—if it attacks their rationality, freedom, relationships with others or their bodily integrity. Certainly, differences can be discerned between these traditions precisely over the priority of these goods. For example, Orthodox Jewish thought emphasizes the sanctity of life (as displayed in bodily integrity) which translates into a stronger commitment to life-extending technologies than in Roman Catholicism, which stresses the capacity for human relationships as a threshold for determining the permissibility of stopping life support.

The monotheistic faiths have also focused a great deal on the legalization of physician assistance in hastening death by providing a terminally ill patient with a lethal prescription of medication. In each instance, arguments supporting physician-assisted suicide have to overcome a long-standing prohibition of suicide. For a variety of reasons, suicide is sinful according to the three traditions. Suicide constitutes a wrong against one's nature and personal dignity ("religious self"). It also harms the community and violates the sovereignty of God. As a result, a physician assisting in suicide may be seen as a moral accomplice in evil, undermining the sacred covenant of the healer.

However, some faith communities in Protestant Christianity and in Reformed Judaism have argued otherwise. When faced with terminal illness, one may well be disposed to ending life, and one's immediate community (or family) may support this method of death. These kinds of arguments stress the dignity of the individual as a free decision-maker (which also applies to persons entrusted with the decision-making responsibilities of others). This dignity provides the basis for a political and philosophical claim to self-determination and opens the possibility for choosing the timing, circumstances and method of one's death. So physicians may be permitted to hasten death by prescribed medications, or even by administering lethal medication. Yet they would never be obligated to do so.

Religious denunciation of euthanasia

Many religious communities have denounced the question of legalizing physician euthanasia, or administrating death. The most vigorous opposition has come from the Roman Catholic tradition, with Pope John Paul II describing euthanasia as an example of the "culture of death" in Western societies. The Pope believes euthanasia is a manifestation of social views that have abandoned the protection of life and lent support to liberalized abortion, capital punishment, and incessant warfare.

In general, much religious opposition is based on concern for patients who may be in vulnerable positions because of their illness or their lack of social and economic resources. There is fear that patients who cannot afford expensive treatment, for example, will be pressured to accept euthanasia. There is also great concern about the moral nature of the doctor's professional self. Islamic teaching, for example, stresses the physician's commitment or covenant to healing. Euthanasia would violate this sacred role.

The spiritual goal of liberation can also be seen as an ethical reason for seeking or hastening death.

Although few in number, there are individual theologians within both the Jewish and Christian traditions for whom euthanasia is not a contradiction but a culmination of religious values such as compassion, mercy, and love. By joining these values to respect for self-determination, some theologians can find a way of tolerating euthanasia as a final resort.

Eastern faith traditions

To die well, say the teachers of eastern religions, one must live well. The views of eastern religious traditions and philosophies have been very influential in global understanding about providing appropriate care to the dying. For example, the pioneering work of the Swiss-born psychiatrist Dr. Elisabeth Kubler-Ross in understanding the experiences of dying patients in Western medical institutions drew directly on understandings of the meaning of "good death" and "stages" in life in Hindu tradition. Buddhist values of compassion, non-violence, and suffering have also influenced the discourse of Western medical ethics. The ethical tension in these two traditions about end-of-life choices is rooted in two main values, liberation and ahimsa (non-violence).

In Hinduism and Buddhism, human beings are captured in endless cycles of rebirth and reincarnation (karma-samsara). The goal of mortal life is detachment from the material world, culminating in the liberation of the true self from the body-mind complex. To experience the good life and the good death, we must be constantly aware of the ultimate trajectory towards liberation.

In both traditions, all living creatures (humans, animals, plants, etc.) represent manifestations of the laws of karmic rebirth. To honour these laws, one must show great respect for the preservation of life and noninjury of sentient beings. Acts destructive of life are morally condemned by the principle of ahimsa, which is the conceptual equivalent of the Western principle of the sanctity of life. In most circumstances ahimsa bears a moral bias towards life-preservation. Yet there is some ethical flexibility which opens the possibility of foregoing treatment or seeking assistance to hasten death.

Perspectives on suicide

As a general rule, both Hinduism and Buddhism oppose suicide as an act of destroying life. However, a distinction is made in both traditions between self-regarding (or self-destructive) reasons and other-regarding (or compassionate) motives for seeking death. To commit suicide over the loss of a child or because of economic hardship (self-regarding reasons) is to commit a morally reprehensible act which reflects the individual's ignorance about the nature of life and human destiny. Instead of achieving the ultimate spiritual goal of liberation, a person who acts in this way will remain trapped in the ongoing karmic cycle of life-death-rebirth. Those who assist in this suicide may also be subject to karmic punishment, for they have violated the principle of ahimsa.

However, a very different perspective emerges when individuals seek death for spiritual motives, of which there are basically two kinds. The first revolves around compassion; concern for the welfare of others as one is dying can be seen as a sign of spiritual enlightenment. So a person can decide to forego treatment to avoid imposing a heavy burden of caregiving on family or friends. He or she may also stop treatment to relieve loved ones of the emotional or economic distress of prolonged dying.

The spiritual goal of liberation can also be seen as an ethical reason for seeking or hastening death. When physical suffering impedes self-control and lucidity, it is permissible to shorten life. Pain or lethargy might cloud the awareness and consciousness at death that both Hindus and Buddhists believe is necessary to ensure a favourable rebirth. Extreme suffering might also cause someone to be so attached to their material life (bodily condition) that they cannot pursue the ultimate spiritual goal of liberation from the material world.

Euthanasia and compassion

This pattern of reasoning—the primacy of spiritual goals of liberation or compassion relative to the preservation of life—also applies to euthanasia through physician injection or administration of a lethal drug. Hindu and Buddhist scholars have found support for this so-called "active" euthanasia in their traditions by reflecting on the meaning of death as a door to liberation, the culmination of life in detachment from the material world. They then go a step further by linking compassion to the norm of self-similitude: "one should act towards others as one would have them act toward oneself". So euthanasia can be seen as a compassionate act or a "mercy killing" for a dying person striving to the highest purpose of human destiny, liberation.

A moral problem arises with euthanasia, however, if the administered medication renders the patient unconscious or unable to comprehend their descent toward death. The patient is unaware precisely at the moment when he or she should be most sensitive and receptive to spiritual teaching and meaning. For these reasons, other modes of bringing about death are preferable morally and religiously.

9

The Media's Positive Portrayal of Euthanasia Is Harmful

Margaret Somerville

Margaret Somerville is an ethicist professor on both the faculty of law and the faculty of medicine at McGill University in Montreal, Canada. She is also the founding director of the McGill Centre for Medicine, Ethics and Law and is active in the worldwide development of bioethics and the study of the wider legal and ethical aspects of medicine and science. Somerville speaks and has published books nationally and internationally, including Death Talk, *from which the following viewpoint was excerpted.*

Much of the debate about euthanasia is carried out in the mass media. Consequently, media ethics and journalists' values shape the public's perceptions of euthanasia. Because of the nature of television, where news stories are expected to have entertainment value, coverage of the euthanasia issue, which requires in-depth consideration, is too often incomplete and one-sided. For example, pro-euthanasia stories where dying people are portrayed pleading for death make dramatic and compelling television stories while anti-euthanasia views which must rely on logic rather than emotion do not. By constantly using death to garner audiences, the media have also numbed the public's reaction to it, making euthanasia more acceptable. The media's presentation of euthanasia has changed the way society views the issue: Rather than believe it is wrong to kill human beings, most Western democracies now believe it is justified to kill people in some circumstances.

I t is not enough, even as an academic, to engage in the euthanasia debate only in academia. This debate must take place primarily in the public square. The media are the messengers—and, they can be the message too. Consequently, the ethics adopted by the mass media, and that govern the content and mode of their communications, will have an im-

Margaret Somerville, *Death Talk: The Case Against Euthanasia and Physician-Assisted Suicide.* Montreal, Canada: McGill-Queen's University Press, 2001. Copyright © 2001 by McGill-Queen's University Press. Reproduced by permission.

portant impact on the outcome of the euthanasia debate.

Canada, like other postmodern, secular, Western democracies, is often called a "media society." People can have very disparate reactions to major controversies—such as euthanasia—depending on whether they learn about them from the mass media or from some other source. One could even come to the conclusion that events perceived through the mass media, especially television, are "more real" and more credible than the same events in real life. Reality at a distance—even virtual reality—has *become* reality; "real reality" has no credibility unless it is authenticated by the mass media. This transference can be called the "mediatization" of controversies. We see them only, or mainly, through the eyes of the mass media.

We can be most attracted to what we most fear, and the mass media provide an infinite number of opportunities to indulge our fear-attraction reaction to death.

Modern technology has meant that debates on important societal issues, such as euthanasia, are not carried out face to face and in person. The "baby boomers" are the first generation for which this has been true, and we have no idea of what the long-term impact on the content and outcomes of these debates might be. Changes caused by mediatization of these debates are important because they deeply affect the "shared story" on which we base our societal paradigm. By that, I mean the store of values, attitudes, beliefs, commitments, and myths that inform collective life (and, therefore, individual lives) and help to give them meaning. Creating a shared story through the mass media could alter the balance among the various components that make up this narrative. In particular, we might engage in too much "death talk" and too little "life talk." We can be most attracted to what we most fear, and the mass media provide an infinite number of opportunities to indulge our fear-attraction reaction to death.

The mass media, especially television, favour some forms of narration, the results of which are woven together to create a shared story. It does not make "good television" to show all the participants in a debate in agreement, especially on some middle-of-the-road opinion. Most television producers choose participants who are polarized, profoundly disagreeing with each other. Moreover, in my experience, most people who work as researchers for the mass media and who screen potential participants are relatively young. Different generations have different views on important societal controversies, especially on important values. My impression is that most mass-media researchers are small-*l* liberals—civil libertarians who defend personal autonomy. This attitude rejects and generates a "pro-choice" world view with respect to abortion, euthanasia, and so on. In the context of religiously based media, however, I have often encountered mass-media researchers who have adopted a clearly "pro-life" world view. It is possible that many media researchers take care not to expose their own positions, adopting whatever stance they believe will elicit the real views of the person they are interviewing. My general experience is that these researchers try to act fairly in choosing a range of people to present their arguments for or against euthanasia. Indeed, their need for conflict to produce good television or radio demands that they do so.

Values and language

At a less personal level, this approach reflects the important traditional journalistic value of objectivity. (It could be argued, however, that objectivity has been supplanted by conflicting aims, such as sensationalism, celebrity, or advocacy.) In achieving objectivity, the choice of interviewees can be a less crucial factor than others, especially when the controversy, as in the case of euthanasia, reflects deep societal tensions. These other factors include decisions as to what is newsworthy and what, therefore, will be covered; the amount of coverage; and, very important, the selection and amount of coverage of related matters. With respect to euthanasia, the quantity and nature of its coverage can be compared with that of pain-relief treatment and the right to refuse treatment or the accessibility of palliative care. The former is given far more attention than the latter. In dealing with euthanasia, then, we need to keep in mind that the mass media make an issue visible (or invisible) and define a "frame" that can determine which related issues are taken into account. And "media reports can set the policy agenda and significantly influence political decisions."

Other factors, which can be only mentioned here, include the language, metaphors, and images that the mass media use. These factors can reflect values, set the tone of debate, trivialize something or render it important, marginalize or empower a different group, define something as an urgent or routine problem, assign blame or innocence, and affect policy and strategy.

Language can be confusing

Language can become confused in the debate over euthanasia. Sometimes, this confusion is accidental; at other times intentional. For example, accidental confusion can be seen in reports that life-support treatment was removed from a brain-dead woman to allow her to die. If she was brain-dead, she was dead. Refusals of treatment that result in death are often innocently—but erroneously—described as euthanasia. . . . Pro-euthanasia advocates equate refusals of treatment and euthanasia and intentionally cause confusion in doing so. They argue that there is no difference between refusals that allow someone to die and euthanasia (a lethal injection); if, they say, the former is ethically and legally acceptable, as most people believe, so is the latter.

The mass media might be reluctant to take stands on some controversies for fear of losing readers or viewers. Some say there was such reluctance in the early days of the AIDS pandemic because this disease was linked with homosexuality and sexual transmission. In this respect, it is interesting to note that the *Globe and Mail*, a national newspaper in Canada, first editorialized on the dangers of euthanasia, but, within a relatively short time, came out in support of it. To act with honesty and integrity, we must be open-minded and courageous enough to be willing to change our views when we decide that we were wrong (much as I was disappointed to see the later stance of the *Globe* and argued against it). But could it also have occurred to the *Globe* that, by adopting these different positions, it could appease *all* its readers—or possibly none of them?

Speaking in the context of AIDS, but in words equally applicable to euthanasia, [sociologist and science commentator] Dorothy Nelkin sums up the power of the mass media to influence us and our values: "The media can move issues to centre stage or keep them out of public view. They serve as filters through which people receive news and interpretations of events. The information they convey, their visual and verbal images, and the tone of their presentation can define the significance of events, shape public attitudes, and legitimate—or call into question—public policies."

Societal issues

On the whole, we have failed to give enough weight to societal issues related to euthanasia. This failure is connected with the mediatization of the euthanasia debate. Sue Rodriguez became a national celebrity in 1993 by taking her case for euthanasia to the Supreme Court of Canada. It made for dramatic television. Here was an articulate, courageous, forty-two-year-old, divorced woman who was dying of amyotrophic lateral sclerosis. She was begging to have euthanasia made available. She was threatening to commit suicide while still able to do so (and thus leave her eight-year-old son even sooner) if she was refused access. The court denied her this right by a majority of five to four, with a plurality of dissenting judgments.

The mass media both reflect and form attitudes.

To capture a reader's or a viewer's attention, the mass media need to personalize stories. This focus makes them resonate in some way with personal experience, especially for those people with experience of the problems being discussed. People need, or at least are perceived to need, personal entries into media presentations. This is one reason why medical stories and medical ethics are so popular in the media: we all strongly identify with the drama of illness, the hope for care and treatment, and the victory of cure. Some stories deal with situations, concepts or abstractions so vast in scope that people feel overwhelmed by the descriptions; these stories show complexities rather than reduce them to readily understood, black-and-white conflicts. This approach is usually described as "academic." It is considered incomprehensible to ordinary people and, consequently, of no interest to them. It causes serious problems in the euthanasia debate—which really does need in-depth, broad-based, consideration in both practical and theoretical terms, if we are to find a wise collective response.

Individualism run wild

The mass media both reflect and form attitudes. This role is relevant to another factor in the euthanasia debate: the impact of the intense individualism of postmodern, secular, Western democracies. It has been described in some instances as individualism run wild. How does individualism play out in the mass media? Rights to autonomy and self-determination are seen by small-*l* liberal researchers and journalists as being almost absolute. Consequently, any infringement on these rights—especially prohibiting access to something, such as euthanasia, that they believe pertains only to the individual—is unacceptable to them, although often they try not to communicate their disapproval to the person they are interviewing. The twentieth-century focus on respect for individual rights has done much good. Taken to an extreme, though, it can do harm that is not offset by any good achieved. Human beings cannot live fully human lives in isolation; they need also to be members of families, groups, communities, and societies. To maintain these forms of connectedness, we must sometimes infringe on the rights of individuals. It is seldom easy to justify this view in the mass media, partly because those justifications are not black and white. They require the balancing of competing benefits, harms, and interests. They often involve difficult and complex value judgments. And they also require the taking into account of societal concerns that are not easy to present in the mass media.

Anti-euthanasia arguments make poor television stories

Some arguments against euthanasia, those based on potential harm to society in both the present and the future, are very much more difficult to present in the mass media than those for euthanasia. Anti-euthanasia arguments do not make dramatic and compelling television. Visual images are difficult to find. We do not personally identify with these arguments in the same way that we do with the pleas of dying people who seek euthanasia. Society cannot be interviewed on television and become a familiar, empathy-evoking figure to the viewing public. Only if euthanasia were legalized and associated with obvious abuses—such as proposals to use it on those who object to it and want to continue living—could we create riveting and gripping images that would be comparable in strength with those projected by Sue Rodriguez in pleading her case for euthanasia and that would adequately communicate the case against euthanasia. Or, perhaps, we need to present the case against euthanasia through the imagination of those who write and read prose and poetry. An example is that in the first chapter of *The Children of Men*, by P.D. James. The author describes the mass death of some old people by euthanasia in the year 2025, a scene that elicits a powerful reaction against euthanasia. . . .

Desensitization to death

It is possible that our reaction to seeing death inflicted has been blunted through the vast exposure to death we are subjected to by the mass media in both news and entertainment programs. This could have overwhelmed our sensitivity to the awesomeness of death and, likewise, of inflicting it. Recent research has shown that human beings have an innate resistance to killing each other and that this is operative even among soldiers in battle—unless they have been systematically desensitized. Could the mass media have desensitized us to death? If so, this is another difficulty in presenting the case against euthanasia in the mass media.

Ironically, among the most powerful ways in which the case *against* euthanasia has been presented on television is through Dr. Jack Kevorkian's [a doctor who has practiced euthanasia many times] efforts to *promote* it. Kevorkian's advocacy has produced a strong negative reaction in many people, including many of those who support euthanasia. Indeed, some of the latter worried that he was damaging the case for euthanasia. A Dutch documentary of a physician providing euthanasia to a terminally ill patient who had requested it was shown on prime-time television in Canada and the United States. It elicited a chill in many viewers. Moreover, it evoked condemnation as exploitation by the mass media of both the patient and of euthanasia itself. Likewise, some people have suggested that, by seeing executions on television, viewers would be so horrified that they would demand the abolition of capital punishment. Disturbingly, it has been pointed out also that the opposite could occur; people might be as fascinated as they were in the past by public executions.

Advocates of legalizing euthanasia can manipulate the mass media to further their cause.

Personal closeness to, or distance from, inflicting death can affect how we perceive our own involvement and that of others in causing someone's death. The mass media can affect our perceptions of closeness by the way in which they present death. This factor of personal closeness distinguishes euthanasia from physician-assisted suicide. Everyone, especially "treating" physicians, can feel more distant from the infliction of death in the latter case than in the former. In the Northern Territory of Australia, where euthanasia was temporarily legalised, a computer-activated "suicide machine" that could be triggered by terminally ill people was developed. It was used for carrying out the first death that took place under that legislation. And even Dutch physicians, with long-term experience in carrying out euthanasia, have recommended that physician-assisted suicide be practised rather than euthanasia, whenever possible; the former is less emotionally stressful for physicians than the latter.

Political correctness

Political correctness is another factor influencing how the mass media deal with euthanasia. Conformity to its dictates is often a consideration in mass-media presentations. This late-twentieth-century concept, which can function as an ideology, articulates and can sensitize us to the rights of some people or groups and the wrongs done to them. But it can also, when taken to extremes, cause harm. One problem is that those who advocate its application sometimes deny that it can cause any harm.

A pro-choice position on euthanasia has been associated with political correctness. Reporting on euthanasia in the *New York Times*, Paul Wilkes quotes Herbert Hendin, a psychiatrist and executive director of the American Suicide Foundation, as follows: "[Euthanasia] became . . . a politically correct issue. . . . [N]o thinking person would be caught talking against [euthanasia] . . . and it became a red badge of courage for liberals . . . to be so enlightened as to be for it. Supposedly, it was the thinking person's decision and statement of their independence so they wouldn't be looked upon as some unthinking, religious fundamentalist." This comment raises the complex issue of the mass media's portrayal of religion and how religion, political correctness, and civil liberties are related (a topic I cannot explore here).

Change and novelty

Consider as well the emphasis on change and novelty in mass-media reporting. It is easy to portray those who uphold traditional values as dinosaurs, lacking the ability to change and soon to become extinct. It is much more difficult to show how one can take important, newer values, such as those developed from concepts of human rights and civil liberties, and incorporate them with older ones. The image that best captures what we need to do is that of a spiral like the DNA helix, not simply a pendulum. A helix allows us to see that, in holding old values, we have not necessarily rejected new perceptions—for instance, those of personal autonomy, self-determination, human dignity, and respect for the individual—but have moved back over old values, taking the new ones with us to find insights that can result from amalgamating them. . . .

Reason and "other ways of knowing"

Western societies have focused, especially in public life, on reason to the exclusion of "other ways of knowing." The pro-euthanasia argument has been based largely on what is presented as a reasoned, utilitarian approach: if people are terminally ill and, therefore, going to die soon anyway, it makes no moral difference—and ought to make no legal difference—if they die naturally or through lethal injection. Yet these arguments are almost invariably presented, . . . in the context of highly emotional interviews with terminally ill people. It is difficult to assess in these situations the extent to which pro-euthanasia responses are elicited by reason or by emotion (especially powerful empathy with suffering people who want euthanasia). Arguments said to be based on reason can seem much easier to present well in the mass media and to be more authoritative than, for instance, those said to be based on moral intuition—important as the latter might be. Those who rely on intuition can seem to be "fuzzy thinkers," moreover, especially when faced with opposition based purely on reason. Reasoned arguments also seem less dependent for their validity on the need to trust and respect the person or the institution that is their source than is the case with arguments based on "other ways of knowing." As individuals and as a society, we have lost trust in authority figures and institutions and, in particular, their exercise of discretion. This means that the kind of latter arguments are unacceptable to many people. . . .

Basic presumptions

Basic presumptions, too, can affect controversies presented in the mass media. If the basic presumption is pro-euthanasia, then those arguing against it have the burden of proof in justifying their position. This could be the current situation. Daniel Callahan, formerly president of the Hastings Center [a bioethics research institute] in New York, sums up the situation as follows: "With physician-assisted suicide, we have a sea change: we are saying it is good, humane and dignified and that it can be handled in some systematic way, free from abuse." In short, we have changed from a society that is based on a presumption that it is wrong to kill people to one that is based on a presumption that it is justified in the case of euthanasia. Has this change been caused by the way in which the issues surrounding euthanasia have been presented in the mass media?

Mass-media ethics

How do we draw the fine line, as ethics requires, between reporting adequately on those seeking euthanasia and allowing the mass media to exploit them in manipulative ways in order to attract public attention, discussion, debate and conflict, and ultimately to increase sales or ratings? In the same way, advocates of legalizing euthanasia can manipulate the mass media to further their cause. And sometimes they can use the dying person primarily for the same purpose. In the case of Sue Rodriguez, that was true of the Right to Die Society of Canada and its president, John Hofsess. After Rodriguez failed to obtain an order from the trial court, which would have allowed her access to physician-assisted suicide or euthanasia, Hofsess immediately went to the mass media and announced that Rodriguez would appeal the ruling. He did so without consulting Rodriguez, who was so angry that she terminated her relationship with him. Subsequently, Hofsess appeared in a CBC television documentary, where he seemed on the verge of tears. Now that he could no longer work for her and her cause, he explained, his life had lost its meaning. He had believed that his efforts on Rodriguez's behalf would be the only actions for which he would be remembered by posterity; that possibility was now destroyed. This admission was an unusually frank, though perhaps unwitting, disclosure of how even well-intentioned public actions, as I am sure was true for Mr. Hofsess, can have many motivations.

Although we cannot make death optional, we can create the illusion that it is by making its timing and the conditions and way in which it occurs a matter of choice.

After this event, Svend Robinson, a federal member of parliament from British Columbia, took up the Rodriguez cause. Robinson is an openly gay politician. In promoting freedom of choice on euthanasia, he reflected very powerfully the political and ideological stance on euthanasia of the gay community in Canada. Robinson stated that he was acting simply as a friend. And, as Lisa Hobbs Birnie and Sue Rodriguez make clear in *Uncommon Will*, Rodriguez was certainly in deep need of friends. Robinson's involvement in the case culminated when he announced in Parliament that he had been present with Rodriguez when she died with the help of a physician. There was widespread debate in the mass media over whether any charges would be laid against him, but none was. . . .

Mass media as forums for "death talk"

We are death-denying, death-obsessed societies in which the many people who no longer adhere to the practice of institutionalized religion have lost their main forums for engaging in "death talk"—namely, their places of religious worship. As humans, we need to engage in death talk if we are to accept as part of life the inevitable reality of death. Arguably, the extensive discussion of euthanasia in the mass media is another forum for contemporary death talk. Instead of being confined to an identifiable location and an hour a week, it has spilled out into the larger world. This exposure makes it more difficult to deny death, because it makes fear of death more pervasive and present. One way to deal with this fear is to believe that we have death under control. The availability of euthanasia can encourage that belief. Euthanasia moves us from chance to choice concerning death. Although we cannot make death optional, we can create the illusion that it is by making its timing and the conditions and way in which it occurs a matter of choice. The availability of euthanasia supports this illusion. By acting as modern forums for death talk, the mass media both elicit expressions of fear of death and seek to deal with them—as do churches by the promise of eternal life. Does this role mean that the mass media are a form of religious institution? After all, the word "religion" simply means binding together. And, in some ways, the mass media cause us to do so. Or is there a difference between people binding together and their cultural homogenization?

Finally, I can attest from personal experience how difficult it was to argue against the pleas of Sue Rodriguez when facing them in the mass media. It was impossible not to empathize deeply with her and her suffering, to admire her courage. I often thought of how societies that, appallingly, still engage in capital punishment give prisoners condemned to death some form of their last wish. But I was not prepared to do this for Rodriguez. She often implicitly asked why I would deny her what she wanted so much and what she saw as the only way to relieve her suffering. My answer was, and still is, that legalizing euthanasia would harm society and diminish the value of respect for human life. It would change the fundamental norm of society—that we must not kill one another—to one that we may do so in some circumstances, albeit for reasons of the utmost mercy and compassion.

In view of all these factors and forces, it is no wonder that the mass media have, and will have, a difficult time in presenting the euthanasia debate fairly, fully, deeply, and wisely, in facilitating and guiding the societal discussion that surrounds it, and, ultimately, in helping us to reach a wise decision about euthanasia.

10

Legalized Euthanasia in the Netherlands Raises Serious Ethical Concerns

Jenny Nolan

Jenny Nolan works as a legislative assistant for the National Right to Life Committee's Department of Medical Ethics.

In the spring of 2001 euthanasia was legalized in the Netherlands, an event that elicited an outcry from many within the nation and around the world. Many saw it as a "sinister trend" that was often practiced without the consent of those being euthanized. In fact, statistics show that 11 to 12 percent of those euthanized in the Netherlands have been put to death without their consent, and only 60 percent of euthanasia cases were reported, although reporting is supposed to be mandatory. The Dutch euthanasia laws are so vague that doctors are expanding the practice to include those who are not terminally ill. For example, doctors euthanized an elderly senator who had no physical illness but felt he was living "a pointless and empty existence." Because of instances such as these, critics fear that the very old, the very young, and the disabled are vulnerable to abuse in the Dutch medical system. Critics also worry that other nations will follow the Dutch example.

Sixty years ago the footsteps of Nazi soldiers drummed through the streets of the Netherlands and swastikas blazed from windows like furious eyes. Hitler's Aktion T4 program, designed to eliminate "life unworthy of life" through euthanasia, was in full swing. Designed to purge the "Aryan race" of congenital defects, it required that hospitals and institutions report patients with disabling or incurable conditions. Across Nazi Europe, physicians killed nearly 100,000 of them.

Evil reigned, but courage lived. In the face of the enemy, Dutch doctors alone, in contrast to every other occupied country, refused to recommend or participate in a single case of euthanasia during World War II. Even Nazi orders not to treat the old or those with little chance of recov-

Jenny Nolan, "Dutch Legalize Euthanasia and Assisted Suicide," *National Right to Life News*, vol. 28, May 2001. Copyright © 2001 by National Right to Life Committee. Reproduced by permission.

ery were disobeyed, according to a famous *New England Journal of Medicine* article written in 1949 by Dr. Leo Alexander.

How times have changed

On April 10 [2001], as an estimated 10,000 Dutch people stood in protest outside The Hague, the Senate voted 46 to 28 to legalize euthanasia. The bill passed the lower house last November [2001] and now awaits only the formality of the [2001] signature of Queen Beatrix to become law.[1] (Like the Queen of England, the monarch of the Netherlands in practice has no discretion to veto laws.)

News of the vote immediately shot across the globe, igniting heated debate on the international scene, but nowhere was the expression of horror more intense than in Germany. The *New York Times* reported, "Front-page newspaper editorials, statements from ministers and criticism from doctors all took the view that, in the words of George Paul Hefty in the *Frankfurter Allgemeine Zeitung* . . . the Dutch had 'breached a dike' with dangerous consequences."

Legally, children as young as 12 may be euthanized with their parents' consent.

Die Welt, a German daily, compared the old Aktion T4 program with the new Dutch law. Under Hitler, "The government thugs that went into institutions for the handicapped to select who was unworthy for life were very careful not to broadcast their intentions. At some level, the old scruples linked to the commandment against killing were present. . . . The scandal in The Hague is that a parliament has imposed a state norm in place of the freedom to uphold such scruples."

The German outcry included those with the most experience in dealing with pain and suffering. The *New York Times* wrote, "German doctors seemed unanimous today in seeing sinister trends behind the Dutch law."

Without explicit request

Dr. Stephen Sahm, a cancer specialist in Wiesbaden, pointed to research suggesting that many of the Netherlands' euthanasia deaths "involve life-ending practices without explicit request." "The process has gained its own dynamics and logic, which is nothing short of merciless," he wrote. "Everyone has the right to a dignified death," said Jarg-Dietrich Hoppe, the president of a leading association of German doctors, "but nobody has the right to be killed. The dangers of abuse are too great."

Dutch courts have favored euthanasia in ever-expanding circumstances in cases going back to 1973. The new law makes legally binding the guidelines that Parliament adopted in 1993. Ostensibly, patients must be undergoing irremediable and unbearable suffering, be aware of all other

---

1. The queen did sign the bill.

medical options, have sought a second professional opinion, and made their request for euthanasia voluntarily, persistently, and independently while being of sound mind.

Legally, children as young as 12 may be euthanized with their parents' consent. Sixteen and 17-year-olds do not need consent, but must have involved their parents or guardians in the decision-making process.

Physicians may not suggest euthanasia, but patients can leave written instructions authorizing it at their physicians' discretion, should the patients become too physically or mentally ill to decide for themselves. All euthanasia cases must be reported to regional review committees.

Proponents lauded the Senate's decision. "We have a good law at last," said Rob Jonquiere, a retired family doctor in the Netherlands who heads the Dutch Association for Voluntary Euthanasia.

He dismissed German criticism, saying, "The Germans have a war trauma and to compare our euthanasia law with what happened in the German past is unacceptable because these methods have nothing to do with each other."

Given that the law is mostly a codification of regulations that have defined the practice of euthanasia in the Netherlands for decades, and that its abuses have been amply demonstrated all along, the assurances from people like Jonquiere that now things are different seem somewhat absurd.

For example, the requirement that the patient be enduring irremediable and unbearable suffering has been interpreted so broadly that [in 2000] an elderly former senator with no significant illness was euthanized solely because he felt he was living a "pointless and empty existence." His doctor was acquitted.

The Netherlands continues to slide deeper into the mentality that death is a cure-all solution.

Speaking independently of that particular case, four days after Parliament's vote legalizing euthanasia in certain circumstances, Health Minister Els Borst declared her readiness to enlarge them. In an April 14 interview, she told a Dutch newspaper that she would not oppose allowing suicide pills for very old people who are healthy.

"Being tired of life has nothing to do with the euthanasia law, with medicine and doctors," Borst said. "You may be releasing someone from their suffering, but it is a suffering that has no link with illness or handicap."

Proponents of euthanasia argue that because a patient's request must be voluntary, there is no danger of people being killed either without their consent or against their expressed wishes to live. But Peter Huurman, a leading opponent, emphasized the weight that falls upon those people who choose to live, and must justify that choice, when euthanasia is a legal and widely acceptable option.

The vulnerable

From a practical standpoint, the Dutch group Cry for Life pointed out that there is no real watchdog standing guard since a doctor has to report euthanasia only after it has been carried out and the main witness can no longer speak. In a press release, Cry for Life claims that recent research shows that 60% of all cases are not reported.

The most vulnerable are the very old, the very young, and those with disabilities. Some 8% of all infants who die in the Netherlands are killed by their doctors, according to a 1997 study published in the British medical journal, *The Lancet.*

In 1991 a Dutch government study found 1,000 cases of euthanasia without patient consent in a total of 8,200 euthanasia deaths that year. A follow-up investigation in 1995 found that number decreased by only .1%.

Taken together, the statistics show that 11–12% of Dutch euthanasia deaths occur without consent. Of the 1995 patients who were killed absent a request for death, 21% were fully competent at the time but 79% were not.

A small, but indomitable, cadre of pro-life forces within Holland is fiercely maintaining the position against euthanasia. Cry for Life, led by Dr. Bert Dorenbos, gathered 40,000 signatures in a last-ditch plea with Parliament not to legalize euthanasia and helped organize the 10,000-person protest in The Hague.

As the bill snaked through the legislative process, members of the Christian party Christenunie and the Christian Democrats, the main opposition party, spoke relentlessly against its passage. Their objections ranged from the practicalities of the bill and its potential to prey on the vulnerable to the overall ethical problem of introducing euthanasia into the normal practice of medicine.

In spite of their efforts, for the moment at least, the Netherlands continues to slide deeper into the mentality that death is a cure-all solution. Other countries are watching. Belgian lawmakers have been drafting an assisted suicide bill for months which they hope to present to both chambers of their parliament later this year.[2]

Following the Dutch vote on April 10, French health minister Bernard Kouchner declared his plans to work toward legalizing euthanasia in France, claiming in a *Reuters* article that there had been an "unquestionable change in French public opinion."[3]

In the United States, Faye Girsh, president of the Denver-based Hemlock Society, hoped for the same result in this country, though she admitted in an *Associated Press* article that it was doubtful the vote in Holland would help win approval for the expansion of assisted suicide in the U.S. Still, "We are very excited," she said. "We have admired what the people of Holland have been doing for the last 20 years."

David N. O'Steen, Ph.D., NRLC executive director, holds another view. "This decision to further codify the current practice of euthanasia is tragic," he stated.

"The so-called new restrictions are little consolation in a country whose justification for euthanasia has slipped inexorably from the terminally ill, to the chronically ill, to the mentally ill, and most recently to those who have no mental or physical illness at all."

2. In 2001 the Belgian Senate passed the bill legalizing physician-assisted suicide; on May 16, 2002, the Belgian House also passed the bill, and it became law on September 22, 2002.   3. As of January 2003, euthanasia was still outlawed in France.

11

Advances in Medical Technology Have Complicated End-of-Life Decisions

C. Lee Parmley

C. Lee Parmley is an associate professor of anesthesiology and critical care and chairman of the department of critical care at the University of Texas M.D. Anderson Cancer Center.

Modern medical technology is keeping patients alive who would have normally died in the past. This situation has given rise to many complex ethical and legal issues. One issue involves the inability of doctors and family members to agree on a definition of "futility"; all concerned must agree when medical treatment appears to be futile before ceasing it, but it is not always clear what constitutes a futile situation. Consequently, using futility as a measure of when to end life is problematic. Disagreements often arise, such as when a physician believes a patient's recovery is hopeless but the patient's family insists on continuing treatment. In these situations, physicians must also consider how much of limited medical resources should be spent on one patient whose outlook is hopeless. A patient's right to determine when treatments should be withdrawn or withheld can be protected by documents such as living will statutes and advance directives. These are written statements of the patient's wishes made ahead of time. However, these statutes and acts do not protect the patient when there are disagreements between the physician and the patient or the patient's surrogate decision maker and the patient's written wishes. These issues and many others point to the need for improved care in end-of-life situations.

With the advances of technology over the past decades, physicians, especially those who practice in the intensive care unit setting, are

C. Lee Parmley, "Ethical Consideration in End-of-Life Medicine," *Internet Journal of Law, Healthcare, and Ethics*, vol. 1, January 2002, p. 1.

increasingly faced with patients who are not going to recover, but who are not going to die due to the application of modern treatment modalities. Development of life-sustaining technology brought about the expansion of the definition of death in the 1970s to include brain death. Some now argue that the definition of death should be further liberalized, while others deem it appropriate to restrict the definition back away from brain death. The concept of medical futility, a hot topic for ethicists, seems to be an outgrowth of our advancements in medical practice. While it is widely accepted that futile treatment should not be provided, many practitioners grapple with the potential for legal ramifications associated with the withdrawal of futile treatment when the very definition of futility seems to be somewhat amorphous.

Unfortunately, medical training often focuses on the sustaining of life with little or no training directed at providing appropriate care for the dying.

Protection and guidance afforded by state living will statutes and natural death acts tend to apply when there is agreement between the physician and the patient or surrogate decision-maker regarding life-sustaining treatment. These statutes may not completely encompass situations where medical futility and disagreement between physician and surrogate decision-maker are involved. The decisions to withhold or withdraw treatment, which is keeping a patient alive, become even more complex when considered in terms of physician-assisted suicide and euthanasia. Physicians must maintain a clear distinction in this regard, as have the courts and most philosophers and ethicists.

Unfortunately, medical training often focuses on the sustaining of life with little or no training directed at providing appropriate care for the dying. The following discussion is an overview of some ethical principles related to death, medical futility, treatment withdrawal and euthanasia. It is intended to provide a very general view of the medico-legal and ethical frontier faced by the practice of modern critical care medicine. For those of us who feel we do a better job of practicing medicine than arguing ethics, it is helpful to work with a relatively simple set of principles and definitions. The four principles of biomedical ethics which tend to be the foundation of our ethical issues in the ICU setting are Beneficence—do some good; Non-maleficence—do no harm; Autonomy—an individual can decide for himself what will be done to his body; and Justice—health care should be allocated fairly to all. When we apply these principles to our challenging ethical situations our discussions will make more sense, and decisions can be reached more easily.

A definition of death

No doubt there was a time when nothing could be clearer than the definition of death; a person was either alive or dead. Based on traditional criteria, the loss of circulatory and respiratory function, death could be declared. Discussions about the stages or process of death tend to progress to a distinction between dying and death. To this discussion is often added consideration of the definition of life, without which there is death. Even when organs are alive and functioning, human life is not sustained in the absence of certain neurologic mechanisms which maintain at least vegetative functions. If these neurologic mechanisms are absent, and the brain is dead, so is the patient. This is true despite the fact that mechanical devices provide support in the absence of neurologic control of the person.

Work started in the late 1960s eventually culminated in the Universal Determination of Death Act which incorporates brain death with death determined by traditional criteria. "An individual who has sustained either (1) irreversible cessation of circulatory and respiratory functions, or (2) irreversible cessation of all functions of the entire brain, including the brain stem, is dead. A determination of death must be made in accordance with accepted medical standards." The concept of brain death is widely accepted, and forms the foundation for organ retrieval for transplantation. Some believe that societal interests in improving health by organ transplantation are sufficient to further expand the concept and definition of brain death.

Brain death is recognized as the loss of whole brain function, including the brainstem. Philosophical arguments based on the unique aspects of human existence would accept a definition of brain death if higher cortical functions are lost despite ongoing brainstem function. Confusion over seemingly optional definitions of death, circulatory death or brain death, has led to the belief that the newer, brain death, definition could be further refined to encompass the permanent cessation of the critical functions of the organism as a whole. Those functions being

1. vital functions of breathing and neurologic control of circulation,
2. integrating functions of physiologic mechanisms that maintain homeostasis, and
3. consciousness, as necessary for a person to maintain hydration, nutrition and protection.

Interestingly, such a definition of death would include individuals existing in a persistent vegetative state (PVS), the most vulnerable of our society, the protection of whom is a significant governmental interest. An evolutionary expansion of brain death, while of ongoing philosophical interest, is not likely to occur in the near future.

Medical futility

In 1994 the Council on Ethical and Judicial Affairs of the American Medical Association (AMA) issued an opinion pertaining to the ethics of futile care. "Physicians are not ethically obligated to deliver care that, in their best professional judgment, will not have a reasonable chance of benefiting their patients. Patients should not be given treatments simply because they demand them. Denial of treatment should be justified by reliance on openly stated ethical principles and acceptable standards of care . . . not on the concept of "futility," which cannot be meaningfully defined." Acceptable standards of care relate to the allocation of limited medical resources, and should consider the likelihood of benefit, urgency of need, change in quality of life, duration of benefit, and, in some cases, the amount of resources required for successful treatment. Also included in acceptable standards should be consideration of the physician's duty to provide adequate health care for society.

The AMA's 1994 ethical opinion regarding futile care is of particular interest in that it seems to be founded on the ethical principles of beneficence and justice, and that it indicates the difficulty in clearly defining futility. In fact, most individuals who choose to discuss medical futility acknowledge the problems in developing a truly accurate and functional definition. Wide definitions include references to the amount of time a life may be saved, the quality of life, the probability of the treatment failing, the costs, and the nonvalidation of treatment not yet proven effective. Narrowly defined, futility can be construed as treatment which is implausible on a physiologic basis.

Physician aid in dying has become a major interest in ethicist circles.

In general, medical futility can be considered care that serves no useful purpose and provides no immediate or long-term benefit, or treatment which even though having physiologic effects, is non-beneficial to the patient as a person. Always surrounding questions of medical futility is the debate over undue physician paternalism and patient autonomy. The potential for imbalance in this area is especially present with the wider definitions of futility, which provide opportunity for the physician's values to essentially override those of the patient.

The allocation of resources

The issue of cost in the determination of medical futility is also problematic. Traditionally discussions regarding the ethical issue of patient care have avoided the matter of a patient's ability to pay for treatment. Certainly a limit must be applied at some point. While the cost of sustaining a single patient may be absorbed by a particular institution, the cost of providing such care for multitudes of such patients would be overwhelming to society. We are challenged to consider whether the use of resources to sustain a seemingly hopeless patient is at the expense of other patients who may receive greater benefit if limited resources were allocated differently. While physicians should participate in development of institutional policies controlling scarce resources, they must remain patient advocates and not make allocation decisions in specific cases. And patients should be informed of the reasoning behind decisions which limit or deny access to resources which are scarce.

In some areas institutional policies have been developed to assist physicians and other health care providers in situations where medical care has become futile. Such policies must be constructed to protect the patient, the institution and the individuals caring for the patient. The ultimate outcome of implementation of a futility policy would likely be withdrawal of treatment deemed to be futile; this over the objection of the patient or more often the patient's family. Many physicians are understandably concerned about such involvement. The withholding or withdrawing of treatment has traditionally been under cover of State living will statutes or natural death acts which presume an agreement between the patient or surrogate and the physician. These statutes fall short of the specific needs brought into play when medical futility is at issue.

Living will statutes and natural death acts

Although lagging behind the needs imposed by ethical issues in modern medicine, living will statutes and natural death acts have been enacted in essentially all states. The Karen Quinlan case in 1976 was a catalyst for development of state laws which would allow patients to formally set forth desires not to be kept alive in the event of terminal illness or permanent unconsciousness. Following the Nancy Cruzan case in 1990, the Federal government enacted the Patient Self-Determination Act which requires all hospitals that accept Federal funds i.e. Medicare, to provide patients with information regarding their rights to refuse treatment.

While virtually all states have enacted either living will statutes or natural death acts, these statutes vary widely from state to state, being shaped by input from interest groups including the right to die and right to life lobbies. Some allow for very powerful documents and others seem to be little more than window dressing without any substantive value. In general these statutes set forth procedures for limitation of treatment, including withholding and withdrawing life-sustaining measures when a patient is terminally ill or suffers an irreversible condition. From a legal perspective, their foundation is the doctrine of informed consent; from an ethical perspective, autonomy.

Natural death acts and living will statutes set forth documentation legally sufficient to establish what is recognized as clear and convincing evidence of what an individual wishes to be done in the event of a specified health situation; a living will or advance directive. The statutes also usually provide for the designation of a surrogate decision-maker. This may be through written documents known as health care power of attorney or durable power of attorney for health care or if no such document has been executed, according to kinship as set forth in the statute.

Physician-assisted suicide is very near active euthanasia, the significant difference being whether a lethal dose of medication is administered by the patient himself or by the physician.

A surrogate can convey the patient's express wishes, if they are known, but if not, decisions to withhold or withdraw life-sustaining treatment are still allowed in some states if such a decision would be consistent with the patient's values as expressed by the surrogate.

The surrogate decision-maker acts on behalf of the incompetent patient under the principle of substituted judgment. The decisions made are to be those that the incompetent patient would make for himself if he were capable of making the decision. In legal terms, this is considered to be a subjective standard. The alternative, objective standard, is applied when decisions are made in what is considered to be the patient's best interest; applying terms such as "reasonable medical judgment," or "what a reasonable person would prefer." The objective and subjective standards differ largely in that the former allows for decisions to be made independent of the patient's desires and personal values; a challenge to the individual's autonomy. Courts find that the constitutional right of privacy, which allows an individual to choose what will be done to his or her body, exists for both competent and incompetent patients, the subjective standard is consistently applied.

Exactly what the incompetent patient would choose at any time may be evident through statements made or written directives. State living will statutes and natural death acts, which set forth procedures for withholding and/or withdrawing life sustaining treatments, vary in the quality of evidence required for surrogate decision making. In the Cruzan case, the state of Missouri's requirement for clear and convincing evidence of a patient's desires was upheld by the U.S. Supreme Court. This high evidentiary standard is not found in most state statutes.

Problems with acts and statutes

Several problems occur with current natural death acts and living will statutes. When an individual executes an advance directive and designates a surrogate through a durable power of attorney for health care, conflicts may arise. The advance directive may clearly indicate the patient's desire not to be sustained in the event of certain irreversible conditions, yet the surrogate's decisions can be inconsistent with this expressed intent. Problems have also occurred when advance directives and documents designating surrogate decision-makers contains specific limitations in precise detail which may ultimately preclude their activation.

Perhaps even more perplexing is the failure of living will statutes and natural death acts to apply in situations of medical futility. Frequently families will insist on continuation of life-sustaining treatment in a hopeless situation. These statutes fail because they rely on the principle of consent for a treatment decision to withhold and/or withdraw life-sustaining treatment, and the family will not agree with such a decision. With interests in promoting ethical interests of beneficence, non-malefecince and justice, many institutions have sought to develop policies to guide physicians faced with situations where futile treatment is demanded.

Withholding, withdrawing, and physician-assisted death

Although uniformity is lacking in States' living will statutes and natural death acts, there is a common general theme; withholding and/or withdrawing treatment which delays natural death is permissible. Some physicians find greater concern in withdrawing than in withholding specific treatments. Essentially though, the same reasons that justify not instituting a treatment also justify stopping it. The fear that treatment cannot be stopped once it is started may even prevent the use of potentially beneficial treatment. Courts and most ethicists find no legal or ethical difference between withholding and withdrawing treatment. This is also the position of the American Medical Association.

Consideration of euthanasia is likely the basis of physician concern over withdrawing treatment and allowing a patient to die naturally. Physician aid in dying has become a major interest in ethicist circles. Those whose arguments support an increasing physician role in assisting with the dying process, seek to eliminate the distinction between allowing a patient to die and actually killing. Many, however, recognize a clear distinction. Likewise, courts delineate a different line of individual rights and interests when considering a patient's right to die as opposed to the autonomous decision to have treatments withheld and/or withdrawn.

Courts identify a fundamental privacy right which constitutionally protects an individual's decisions about what will be done to his body, encompassing the right to refuse treatment which will sustain life. In cases which have addressed the issue of physician-assisted suicide, courts have relied on a lesser, liberty interest, in the recognition of an individual's right to control the time and manner of death. Presumably this rationale will be applied in the cases expected to flow from Oregon's 1997 Death With Dignity Act, as increasing physician assistance in patient death is seen.

Types of euthanasia

Physician-assisted suicide is very near active euthanasia, the significant difference being whether a lethal dose of medication is administered by the patient himself, or by the physician. In consideration of euthanasia, a physician's withdrawal or withholding of life-sustaining medical treatment in accordance with a patient's wishes falls within the definition of voluntary passive euthanasia. It is permissible to administer comfort medications to such patients, even if the medication may also compromise vital functions, which could ultimately hasten death (double effect). By contrast if the same medication is administered specifically to hasten the patient's death, the process becomes active euthanasia.

Understandably the entire patient-assisted suicide issue is seen by many as a slippery slope. Without sufficient regulation the risk to vulnerable members of society may be great, and clearly not all physicians will choose to participate in this aspect of medical practice. Concerns on this frontier, however, should not impair the capability to provide medical care at the end of life in a non-maleficent way, with due recognition of patient autonomy.

Proper care for dying patients

The capability of modern medicine and technology to keep patients alive has pressed physicians into an era where the very goals of medicine must be reviewed and perhaps revised. Patients who clearly would have died in prior decades now can survive; some but not all of whom being fully restored to normal functional existence. American society adapts to and accepts many of those with less than full recovery; buildings are modified with ramps, special parking spaces and rest rooms. At some level, however, survival is not associated with function recovery, or ultimately survival itself without the assistance of artificial means cannot be expected.

American society and medical practitioners must focus on this area, anticipating and shaping the changes that will occur.

Medical practice, which has progressed so well in answering the question of "How can we keep patients alive?" must now better answer the question "How should we allow patients to die and properly care for them?" In doing this we must remember our ethical duty to offer and provide only that care which is of benefit, not harmful, allowing patients to retain their decision-making right, while remaining mindful of our societal responsibility to maintain a level of care which can be available for all.

Organizations to Contact

The editors have compiled the following list of organizations concerned with the issues debated in this book. The descriptions are derived from materials provided by the organizations. All have publications or information available for interested readers. The list was compiled on the date of publication of the present volume; the information provided here may change. Be aware that many organizations take several weeks or longer to respond to inquiries, so allow as much time as possible.

American Foundation for Suicide Prevention (AFSP)
120 Wall St., Twenty-second Floor, New York, NY 10005
(888) 333-AFSP • (212) 363-3500 • fax: (212) 363-6237
website: www.afsp.org

The foundation supports scientific research on depression and suicide, educates the public and professionals on the recognition and treatment of depressed and suicidal individuals, and provides support programs for those coping with the loss of a loved one to suicide. It opposes the legalization of physician-assisted suicide. AFSP publishes a policy statement on physician-assisted suicide and the quarterly newsletter *Lifesavers.*

American Life League
PO Box 1350, Stafford, VA 22555
(540) 659-4171
e-mail: sysop@all.org • website: www.all.org

The league believes that human life is sacred. It works to educate Americans on the dangers of all forms of euthanasia and opposes legislative efforts that would legalize or increase its incidence. It publishes the bimonthly pro-life magazine *Celebrate Life;* videos; brochures, including *Euthanasia and You* and *Jack Kevorkian: Agent of Death;* and newsletters monitoring abortion- and euthanasia-related legal developments.

American Society of Law, Medicine, and Ethics (ASLME)
765 Commonwealth Ave., Suite 1634, Boston, MA 02215
(617) 262-4990 • fax: (617) 437-7596
e-mail: aslme@bu.edu • website: www.aslme.org

ASLME works to provide scholarship, debate, and critical thought to professionals concerned with legal, health care, policy, and ethical issues. It publishes the *Journal of Law, Medicine, and Ethics* as well as a quarterly newsletter.

Compassion in Dying (CID)
6312 SW Capital Hwy., Suite 415, Portland, OR 97239
(503) 221-9556 • fax: (503) 228-9160
e-mail: info@compassionindying.org • website: www.compassionindying.org

CID believes that dying patients should receive information about all options at the end of life, including those that may hasten death. It provides information on intensive pain management, comfort or hospice care, and humane, effective aid in dying. CID advocates laws that would make assistance in dying legally available for terminally ill, mentally competent adults, and it publishes a newsletter detailing these efforts.

Dying with Dignity
55 Eglinton Ave. East, Suite 705, Toronto, ON M4P 1G8 Canada
(800) 495-6156 • (416) 486-3998 • fax: (416) 489-9010
e-mail: info@dyingwithdignity.ca • website: www.dyingwithdignity.ca

Dying with Dignity works to improve the quality of dying for all Canadians in accordance with their own wishes, values, and beliefs. It educates Canadians about their right to choose health care options at the end of life, provides counseling and advocacy services to those who request them, and builds public support for voluntary physician-assisted dying. Dying with Dignity publishes a newsletter and maintains an extensive library of euthanasia-related materials that students may borrow.

End of Life Choices
PO Box 101810, Denver, CO 80250-1810
(800) 247-7421 • (303) 639-1202 • fax: (303) 639-1224
e-mail: hemlock@hemlock.org • website: www.endoflife.org

End of Life Choices is the website of the Hemlock Society, which believes that terminally ill individuals have the right to commit suicide. The society publishes books on suicide, death, and dying, including *Final Exit*, a guide for those suffering with terminal illness and considering suicide. The society also publishes the newsletter *TimeLines*.

Euthanasia Research and Guidance Organization (ERGO)
24829 Norris Ln., Junction City, OR 97448-9559
(541) 998-1873 • fax: (541) 998-1873
e-mail: ergo@efn.org • website: www.assistedsuicide.org

ERGO provides information and research findings on physician-assisted dying to persons who are terminally or hopelessly ill and wish to end their suffering. Its members counsel dying patients and develop ethical, psychological, and legal guidelines to help them and their physicians make life-ending decisions. The organization's publications include *Deciding to Die: What You Should Consider* and *Assisting a Patient to Die: A Guide for Physicians*.

Human Life International (HLI)
4 Family Life Ln., Front Royal, VA 22630
(540) 635-7884 • fax: (540) 636-7363
e-mail: hli@hli.org • website: www.hli.org

HLI categorically rejects euthanasia and believes assisted suicide is morally unacceptable. It defends the rights of the unborn, the disabled, and those threatened by euthanasia, and it provides education, advocacy, and support services. HLI publishes the monthly newsletters *HLI Reports*, *HLI Update*, and *Deacons Circle*, as well as online articles on euthanasia.

International Anti-Euthanasia Task Force (IAETF)
PO Box 760, Steubenville, OH 43952
(740) 282-3810
e-mail: info@iaetf.org • website: www.iaetf.org

The task force opposes euthanasia, assisted suicide, and policies that threaten the lives of the medically vulnerable. IAETF publishes fact sheets and position papers on euthanasia-related topics in addition to the bimonthly newsletter *IAETF Update*. It analyzes the policies of and legislation concerning medical and social work organizations and files amicus curiae briefs in major "right-to-die" cases.

National Right to Life Committee (NRLC)
512 10th St. NW, Washington, DC 20004
(202) 626-8800
e-mail: nrlc@nrlc.org • website: www.nrlc.org

The committee is an activist group that opposes euthanasia and assisted suicide. NRLC publishes the monthly *NRL News* and the four-part position paper "Why We Shouldn't Legalize Assisting Suicide."

Oregon Death with Dignity National Center
520 SW Sixth Ave., Suite 1030, Portland, OR 97204
(503) 228-4415 • fax: (503) 228-7454
e-mail: info@dwd.org • website: www.dwd.org

This is a new site that combines the former Death with Dignity National Center (DDNC) with the Oregon Death with Dignity (ODWD) site. The goal of the Oregon Death with Dignity National Center is to promote a comprehensive, humane, responsive system of care for terminally ill patients. It publishes a variety of information, including the pamphlet *Making Choices at the End of Life*.

Partnership for Caring
1620 Eye St. NW, Suite 202, Washington, DC 20006
(202) 296-8071 • fax: (202) 296-8352
e-mail: pfc@partnershipforcaring.org • website: partnershipforcaring.org

The Partnership for Caring is a national nonprofit organization that partners individuals and organizations together to improve how people die in the United States. Among other services, Partnership for Caring operates the only national crisis and information hotline dealing with end-of-life issues, and provides state-specific living wills and medical powers of attorney (also called advance directives).

Bibliography

Books

Raphael Cohen-Almagor — *The Right to Die with Dignity: An Argument in Ethics, Medicine, and Law.* Piscataway, NJ: Rutgers University Press, 2001.

Ian Dowbiggen — *A Merciful End: The Euthanasia Movement in Modern America.* New York: Oxford University Press, 2003.

Gerald Dworkin, Sissela Bok, and R.G. Frey — *Euthanasia and Physician-Assisted Suicide: For and Against.* New York: Cambridge University Press, 1998.

Kathleen M. Foley — *The Case Against Assisted Suicide: For the Right to End-of-Life Care.* Baltimore: Johns Hopkins University Press, 2002.

John M. Freeman and Kevin McDonnell — *Tough Decisions.* New York: Oxford University Press, 2001.

Daniel Hillyard and John Dombrink — *Dying Right: The Death with Dignity Movement.* New York: Routledge, 2001.

Derek Humphry — *Final Exit: The Practicalities of Self-Deliverance and Assisted Suicide for the Dying.* New York: Delta, 2002.

Derek Humphry and Mary Clement — *Freedom to Die.* New York: St. Martin's, 1998.

Michael J. Hyde — *The Call of Conscience: Heidegger and Levinas, Rhetoric and the Euthanasia Debate.* Columbia: University of South Carolina Press, 2001.

Roger S. Magnusson — *Angels of Death: Exploring the Euthanasia Underground.* New Haven, CT: Yale University Press, 2002.

Cedric A. Mims — *When We Die: The Science, Culture, and Rituals of Death.* New York: St. Martin's, 1999.

M. Scott Peck — *Denial of the Soul: Spiritual and Medical Perspectives on Euthanasia and Mortality.* New York: Three Rivers, 1998.

Jodi Picoult — *Mercy.* New York: Pocket Books, 2001.

David Rabe and Richard Selzer — *A Question of Mercy.* Berkeley, CA: Grove, 1998.

Fiona Randall and R.S. Downie — *Palliative Care Ethics.* New York: Oxford University Press, 1999.

Betty Rollin — *Last Wish.* Boulder, CO: PublicAffairs, 1998.

Jennifer M. Scherer and Rita J. Simon	*Euthanasia and the Right to Die: A Comparative View.* Boulder, CO: Rowman & Littlefield, 1999.
Wesley J. Smith	*Culture of Death: The Assault on Medical Ethics in America.* San Francisco: Encounter Books, 2000.
Lois Snyder and Arthur L. Caplan, eds.	*Assisted Suicide: Finding Common Ground.* Bloomington: Indiana University Press, 2001.
Maurice Steinberg and Stuart J. Youngner, eds.	*End-of-Life Decisions: A Psychological Perspective.* Arlington, VA: American Psychiatric Press, 1998.
Michael M. Uhlmann, ed.	*Last Rights: Assisted Suicide and Euthanasia Debated.* Grand Rapids, MI: William B. Eerdmans, 1998.

Periodicals

Tom L. Beauchamp	"The Medical Ethics of Physician-Assisted Suicide," *Journal of Medical Ethics*, December 1999.
David Boonin	"How to Argue Against Active Euthanasia," *Journal of Applied Philosophy*, 2000.
Daniel Callahan	"Defending the Sanctity of Life," *Society*, July/August 2001.
Glenn Carlson	"Neuromuscular Blockade Administration to End Suffering: An Ethical Dilemma," *Critical Care Nursing Quarterly*, November 1999.
John Cloud	"A License to Kill?" *Time*, April 23, 2001.
Mark Crane	"The Latest Malpractice Risk: Saving Your Patient's Life," *Medical Economics*, February 23, 1998.
Len Doyal and Lesley Doyal	"Why Active Euthanasia and Physician-Assisted Suicide Should Be Legalised," *British Medical Journal*, November 10, 2001.
Economist	"Last Rights," November 17, 2001.
Ezekiel Emanuel	"Assisted Suicide Largely Shunned," *Christian Century*, December 6, 2000.
Sharon I. Fraser and James W. Walters	"Death—Whose Decision? Euthanasia and the Terminally Ill," *Journal of Medical Ethics*, April 2000.
Gere B. Fulton and Joseph J. Fins	"Removing the Mask," *Hastings Center Report*, March/April 2003.
Raanan Gillon	"When Doctors Might Kill Their Patients," *British Medical Journal*, May 29, 1999.
Faye Girsh	"Death with Dignity: Choices and Challenges," *USA Today*, March 2000.
Daniel Gorman	"Active and Passive Euthanasia: The Cases of Drs. Claudio Alberto de la Rocha and Nancy Morrison," *Canadian Medical Association Journal*, March 23, 1999.
Amy Haddad	"Ethics in Action," *RN*, March 2000.

John Harris   "Consent and End of Life Decisions," *Journal of Medical Ethics*, February 2003.

C.W. Henderson   "Study: Terminally Ill Cancer Patients Favor a Legalization of Euthanasia and Physician-Assisted Suicide," *Cancer Weekly*, September 19, 2000.

Human Life Review   "Did They Murder My Dad?" Spring 1998.

John F. Kavanaugh   "Euthanizing Life," *America*, May 7, 2001.

Howard L. Kaye   "On Moral Blindness," *Society*, July/August 2001.

Nelson Lund   "Why Ashcroft Is Wrong on Assisted Suicide," *Commentary*, February 2002.

Janis Moody   "Euthanasia: A Need for Reform," *Nursing Standards*, November 15, 2002.

Susana Nuccetelli and Gary Seay   "Relieving Pain and Foreseeing Death: A Paradox About Accountability and Blame," *Journal of Law, Medicine, and Ethics*, Spring 2000.

Terry O'Neill   "Thou Shalt Dispense Death," *Report/Newsmagazine*, April 24, 2000.

Anna Quindlen   "In a Peaceful Frame of Mind," *Newsweek*, February 2, 2002.

Andrea E. Richardson   "Death with Dignity," *Humanist*, July/August 2002.

Jeff Sharlet   "Why Are We Afraid of Peter Singer?" *Chronicle of Higher Education*, March 10, 2000.

Peter Singer   "Changing Ethics in Life and Death Decision Making," *Society*, July/August 2001.

Index